REGENCY PATRON:
SIR GEORGE BEAUMONT

by the same author

*

THE BLAZON OF HONOUR—
A STUDY IN RENAISSANCE MAGNANIMITY

1. *Sir George Beaumont*, by John Hoppner

REGENCY PATRON:
SIR GEORGE BEAUMONT

by Margaret Greaves

METHUEN & CO LTD
11 New Fetter Lane · London EC4

First published in 1966
by Methuen & Co Ltd
11 *New Fetter Lane, London EC4*
© *Margaret Greaves* 1966
Printed in Great Britain by
the Shenval Press, Hertford and Harlow

FOR

MICK AND MARY

Contents

9

Illustrations

11

Foreword

This book makes no claim to be an exhaustive biography of Sir George Beaumont. Its aim is to show certain aspects of Regency life and taste, revealed through the experiences of a well-known patron whose friendship was shared by poets, painters, scientists, men of affairs, persons of fashion, and connoisseurs of the arts. There are contemporary sources for all detail given, however trivial, but I have deliberately selected from the available material, so that my main theme may remain clear. I have confined myself almost entirely to published sources, but I have to thank the Marquis of Normanby for his generous permission to make use of private letters in the possession of his family.

Birthright of a Country Gentleman

The year is 1812. The news has just reached England that
the Russians have fired Moscow rather than allow Napoleon
to use it as a winter headquarters for his army. The yeomanry
are training earnestly in many an English village, their in-
expert manoeuvres watched by the inhabitants with mingled
pride and apprehension. Nervous ladies listen to rumours of
French landings in Wales and bread riots in Lancashire, and
nightly barricade their doors with the fire irons. And on the
last day but one of October, in the mild warmth of an autumn
noon, a pretty sentimental scene is being enacted in a Leicestershire garden, as if there were never a ripple of disturbance
in the whole of Europe.

Four slightly elderly persons are engaged in laying a
foundation stone. The slim and elegant woman, whom the
years still touch lightly, is Lady Beaumont; and beside her
stands her husband, that distinguished patron and amateur
of the arts, Sir George Howland Beaumont, baronet, of
Coleorton Hall. With them are their two guests, both
greatly respected members of the Royal Academy, Joseph
Farington and William Owen. Sir George handles the
trowel first, followed by the others. When the stone is
duly laid, each member of the party strikes it with a
small mallet, Lady Beaumont declaiming clearly as she
does so: 'May nothing but Time destroy this monument.'
The local workmen, assembled to attend the little cere-
mony, look stolidly on. They are accustomed to a world in
which the gentry have their romantic fancies, and must be
indulged in their whims and eccentricities; and they have
no notion that this simple and charming ritual marks the

end of an era. Even the gentry themselves are very little aware of it.

The foundation stone is that of a monument to Sir Joshua Reynolds, of all eighteenth-century artists the most at one with his period. It is to stand in the scented shade of an avenue of limes, although at present the trees are still small and young. They were planted six years ago as part of the newly established garden planned by that rather modern poet, William Wordsworth, in which the classic serenity of an eighteenth-century landscape garden has been modified by a more recent and picturesque taste. Mr Wordsworth has already written the verses which are to be inscribed upon the stone:

> *Ye Lime-trees, ranged before this hallowed Urn,*
> *Shoot forth with lively power at Spring's return;*
> *And be not slow a stately growth to rear*
> *Of pillars, branching off from year to year,*
> *Till they have learned to frame a darksome aisle; –*
> *That may recall to mind the awful Pile*
> *Where Reynolds, 'mid our country's noblest dead,*
> *In the last sanctity of fame is laid.*
> *– There, though by right the excelling Painter sleep*
> *Where Death and Glory a joint sabbath keep,*
> *Yet not the less his spirit would hold dear*
> *Self-hidden praise, and Friendship's private tear:*
> *Hence, on my patrimonial grounds have I*
> *Raised this frail tribute to his memory;*
> *From youth a zealous follower of the Art*
> *That he professed; attached to him in heart;*
> *Admiring, loving, and with grief and pride*
> *Feeling what England lost when Reynolds died.*

The trees are growing as fast as they can upon the patrimonial grounds: and eleven years later, when they have grown high enough to arch above the cenotaph, and another autumn has turned their leaves to a glow, the scene is to be painted by Constable as he quietly works a revolution in

English painting. The moment must have passed as briefly and smoothly as the thin October sunshine: yet, within it, traditional painting, traditional poetry, traditional landscape, met those of a new world.

The name of Sir George Beaumont, chief actor in this little scene, slips in and out of the personal records of late Georgian and Regency England, and of later histories of romantic literature and art, without gaining much attention from a modern reader – a gross instance of national ingratitude to the man who above all others was responsible for the founding of the National Gallery, and whose beneficence relieved the material anxieties of many whose works we still cherish. Time has indeed spared the monument, which still stands within its darksome aisle, but has undone the memory of the two who raised it.

It is a pity that Jane Austen and the Beaumonts appear not to have known of each other, although she was probably engaged on *Mansfield Park* while Sir George was planning his Reynolds cenotaph. He would have enjoyed her novels had he read them; and she would have found in him a hero after her own heart, among the cross-currents of a group of people as interesting and sometimes as absurd as any she ever invented. Many a time, reading the letters of Beaumont and his friends, one has an entertaining illusion of being in a world of Jane Austen's own creation. Though his rank is rather higher than that with which she usually cares to meddle, and his fortune greater, he often reminds us of a Mr Darcy without his reserve or a Mr Knightley with more sophisticated elegance; Sir Walter Elliott would have coveted his acquaintance, and Sir George would have evaded him with civilly disguised distaste. But in one thing she would not have followed him; she knew nothing of the world of art which was the dominating interest of his life.

Beaumont was not only an amateur artist of some repute in his own day. He was also one of the most generous and delicate-minded, and one of the last, of the long line of English patrons. 'Is not a patron,' asked Johnson, out of the bitterness of his own experience, 'one who looks with unconcern on a man struggling for his life in the water, and, when he has reached the ground, encumbers him with help?' He is 'commonly a wretch who supports with insolence, and is paid with flattery'. But Crabbe, on the very verge of defeat and starvation, with as yet nothing at all to commend him beyond his confidence in himself, found in Burke the most generous and faithful of benefactors. He pays public tribute of gratitude to his patron, nearly forty years later, in his preface to the *Borough*:

> Of his private worth, of his wishes to do good, of his affability and condescension; his readiness to lend assistance when he knew it was wanted, and his delight to give praise where he thought it was deserved; of these I may write with some propriety. . . . He delighted to give encouragement to any promise of ability, and assistance to any appearance of desert.

The eighteenth century must have bred many of both kinds; but, for good or ill, the private patron was wholly necessary to writers and artists alike. The church had long ceased to employ painters; the general public had no means of access to their works. There was no process of reproduction other than an engraver's copy, and it was late in the century before English engraving commanded any respect compared with foreign work. Without the individual wealthy purchaser the artist must have painted in vain for a living. The patron not only enabled the artist to live; he established his reputation by the generosity with which he shared his treasures with others as much as by the cachet which his name and title conferred upon the purchase. He could display his acquisitions chiefly in London, whither then, as now, anyone who hoped for fame or fortune was sure to gravitate sooner or later. Anyone even in the most modest circumstances could obtain permission to visit the collections in the great private houses, if he could first get a suitable introduction. Visitors fortunate enough to gain the entrée to the artistic circle would be driven in their host's carriage to view the collections of Beaumont or the banker Angerstein,[1] or the even greater one of the Marquis of Stafford, or to see a picture known to be in the hands of a dealer or being copied in an artist's studio. Thus the patron helped the new artist to make his bow to the world, and at the same time made available to him the great pictures of the past which he could otherwise never have seen except in monochrome engravings. The patron became the intermediary between tradition and experiment. He would even lend his pictures to be studied by an artist or copied for practice by students of the Royal Academy. In the great country houses, too, the interested tourist was welcome to see the owner's possessions. Even as late as the Regency, when Elizabeth Bennet and her uncle and aunt visited Pemberley, the housekeeper took them to the picture gallery as a matter of course.

Without such courtesies from their patrons, artists would hardly have become known beyond the confines of their own narrow circle. Wordsworth, writing to thank Sir George Beaumont for the gift of Reynolds' *Discourses*, confessed that 'never having had an opportunity of *studying* any pictures whatsoever, I can be but a very inadequate judge'. The eighteenth-century artist might create pictures, but without a patron he would remain obscure, and would starve if he still insisted on painting; while the eighteenth-century writer was only a little less dependent. He might find someone to print his works, and a small circle of readers to buy them. He did indeed feel rather more independent than the artist, and for that reason was more quickly susceptible to intellectual change. But the reading public was still so small that very few could

---

[1] John Julius Angerstein (1735–1823), merchant banker, philanthropist, and art collector. Of Russian extraction, he came to England when fifteen, became an underwriter at Lloyd's, and eventually gained a vast fortune. After his death his pictures were bought for the nation. Among many worthy actions he obtained an Act of Parliament which prevented owners from changing the name of a ship – a practice often used to disguise unseaworthy vessels.

hope to live entirely by the pen without the help afforded by some approving benefactor – whether from a real love of letters or a desire to shine as a local Maecenas. Some may indeed have 'supported with insolence', but most were conscientiously performing one of the duties expected of a man of rank and taste. And if, in return for the money and reputation they could bestow upon their protégés, some patrons hankered after the pleasures of acknowledged connoisseurship, who shall blame them?

Certainly the patron still reigned supreme in the world of English taste when George Howland Beaumont was born at Great Dunmow in Essex on November 6, 1753; and he could hardly have entered life at a more propitious moment for one of his disposition. Endowed with natural taste and genuine talent, with the warmth and charm and tact which drew others to him, and with birth and fortune to give him sufficient ascendancy, he was inevitably destined to be a patron. The combination of gifts was as happy for himself as for the many he was to befriend. He was born, like Beatrice, under a dancing star.

His birth was hardly likely to cause much of a stir outside his own family, for the Beaumonts were not among those who 'could jog on with a moderate income of £40,000 a year', though their lineage was more ancient than that of many who crowded the rooms at St James's. His father belonged to a younger branch of one of the oldest families in England, descended from the union of a son of a twelfth-century King of Jerusalem and Berengaria, Princess of Castille, with Agnes, Viscountess de Beaumont and Mayne, whose great-grandmother was a natural daughter of Henry I of England (a distinction no doubt shared with a number of other great families). Among their ancestors the Beaumonts counted Alexander Comyn, Earl of Buchan; and later a fourteenth-century Knight of the Garter, whose son – Sir Thomas Beaumont, knight, Lord of Basqueville in France – was also Warden of the Cinque Ports and Governor of Dover Castle.

This Sir Thomas married Philippa, the daughter and heir of
Thomas Maureward, esquire, of Overton Quartermarch, later
known as Coleorton, deep in the Leicestershire forest of
Charnwood where 'a wren and a squirrel might hop from tree
to tree for six miles; and in summer time a traveller could
journey from Beaumanoir to Burden, a good twelve miles,
without seeing the sun'. Here Beaumonts were to live for
another four centuries, and our Sir George was to make it in
the course of time the home of his happiest years. Close by
was the ancient nunnery of Grace Dieu, granted to one of the
family in Henry VIII's reign, and later the home of Francis
Beaumont, the Elizabethan dramatist. It is of this that Thomas
Bancroft wrote in 1639:

> *Grace-Dieu, that under Charnwood stand'st alone,*
> *As a grand relicke of religion,*
> *I reverence thine old, but fruitfull worth,*
> *That lately brought such noble Beaumonts forth,*
> *Whose brave heroicke Muses might aspire*
> *To match the anthems of the heavenly quire.*

In each generation there were Beaumonts who served their
country with honour, and often with distinction. The little
church at Coleorton still shelters the magnificent marble
tomb of Sir Henry Beaumont, knight of the shire for Leicestershire, and of Elizabeth, his wife. A younger brother of this
Sir Henry acquired by marriage the lordship of Stoughton,
some twenty-five miles away; and it was a younger son of
this branch of the Leicestershire family, William Beaumont,
who came to live in Great Dunmow in 1760. Another brother,
Thomas, followed him eight years later and became vicar of
the parish. Possibly William Beaumont already had some
interests in Essex, for there were Beaumonts living in the
Hundred of Dedham and in other parts of the county who
claimed that they also were in some way descended from the
Leicestershire family.

William Beaumont must have settled in Dunmow as a

simple country gentleman, whose son – another William – would have expected little of fortune beyond a sufficient income, an honoured name, and the quiet life of a country squire. This second William died young, leaving his two-year-old son, George, to succeed him. But through George the family connection with Leicestershire was once again renewed. His distant cousin, Thomas, Viscount Beaumont of Swords, had left the Coleorton estates in entail, first to his own brother, Sir Lewis Beaumont, and then to George. The boy was only twelve when on Sir Lewis's death he succeeded to the baronetcy and the Leicestershire property, the Viscounty having ceased with Thomas.

Eventually the new Sir George visited Coleorton and took some interest in it, but his heart remained in the Essex countryside where he was born. There was little to attract him in the plain undistinguished house which had been built soon after the Civil War on the site of the old manor. The property had been neglected, for no Beaumont had lived in it since the death of the last Viscount in 1702. Sir George continued to let it while he himself preferred to live in his father's house in Dunmow – a small, beautiful manor in Elizabethan brick. It was rambling and rather inconvenient inside, 'with nothing remarkable but its awkward passages', as Coleridge was later to complain; but it stood high, by the standards of that flat county, above a slope of green fields falling away to the little church below and the soft pastoral country beyond it. Above it stretched a further gentle hill, known as Beaumont Hill even to this day; and a mile of doubtful road – Dunmow Causeway – separated it from the village. Chapman and André's map of 1777 marks it as Brick House, but it came later to be called the Clock House because of the curious clock tower above the entrance. It was a very proper seat for a country gentleman. The new Sir George's roots were here rather than in Leicestershire, and he strengthened the tie still further by marriage. It was a marriage of common sense and prudence, an alliance with an unpreten-

2. *The Clock House, Dunmow, as it is today*

3. *Gracedieu Priory*, by Sir George Beaumont

4. *The Earl of Mulgrave, Sir George Beaumont, General Phipps, and the Hon. Augustus Phipps*, by John Jackson

tious but securely established local family, the Howlands of Stonehall. The Dunmow parish registers of the first half of the century suggest that they were rising in importance: various Howlands are at first recorded by their name alone, then with the addition of 'Gent' and finally that of 'Esquire'. They owned a very comfortable property on the far side of Dunmow, one of its boundaries dividing it from the much greater one of Easton Lodge, the seat of Lord Maynard. Through an earlier marriage they also had an interest in the Haverhill estate of the Coldhams, another local family of substance. It was an eminently suitable choice. Sir George's bride, Rachel, was the youngest of the eight children of Mr Charles Howland of Stonehall; but although she was thirty-three at the time, and four years older than her husband, there is no need to suppose a marriage of mere convenience. Later evidence suggests that she was a woman capable of inspiring deep and lasting affection in her family and friends. Coleridge was years later to describe her even at eighty-six as 'a sort of miracle for beauty, and clear understanding and cheerfulness'.

Two years later Rachel presented her husband with an heir, who took both his father's name and that of her own family. Two other sons were born, but both died in infancy, and the father himself lived only a few years longer. He died on February 4, 1762, aged thirty-six, leaving behind him his nine-year-old son as Sir George Howland Beaumont of Dunmow and of Coleorton in the county of Leicestershire.

Young Sir George had all his father's love for his Essex home, and much affection for all his Howland relations, but even in his boyhood Coleorton seems to have had a romantic attraction for him. Years later he talked to Wordsworth of his early love for the place. He must have visited it sometimes, for his father had been High-Sheriff of Leicestershire in the last year of his life, and it had associations enough to stir the heart of a romatically-minded boy – the ancient ruins of Grace Dieu, the renown of Francis Beaumont, the great marble tomb of his ancestors, all combining to quicken that pride in his race and history which he felt throughout his life. But he still lived on with his mother in the Clock House, leaving Coleorton in the care of agents appointed by his father – unfortunately, as it proved, for the older Sir George had been no judge of character. His chief agent was incompetent and his under-agent a rogue, but it was years before their new employer was to discover it.

Indeed there was little reason why he should find it out too soon, in that remote world on the far side of the railway revolution. Our generation prides itself, if rather apprehensively, on the annihilation of space, although it can make little real difference whether Europe and America are three weeks or three hours apart when once the habit of travel is taken for granted. Much greater in its effects was that less spectacular revolution of September 15, 1830, when the first steam-operated railway passenger line was opened between Liverpool and Manchester. The England of Sir George Beaumont's lifetime, on the far side of that event, is so strange to most of us that we find it difficult to imagine among the evidences of what seems otherwise so modern a society. Outside London, Bristol, and Birmingham, and perhaps a dozen other towns of considerable size, lay a world of small country towns, remote hamlets, and isolated farmsteads – self-contained communities almost as undisturbed by the outer world as they had been for centuries past. One is only surprised at how far and how frequently the gentry *did* travel, in their own coaches or by post-chaise; while for humbler people in the mid-century there was only the occasional carrier's cart. Sir George was more than thirty before the first mail coaches began to run, astonishing everyone by their magnificent speed of six miles an hour. Then at last Dunmow had its own public service, proudly reported in the *Universal British Directory*. A diligence left the Saracen's Head Inn three times a week, at seven in the morning, to join the Stortford coach at Harlow, fourteen miles away, and returned at five in the afternoon of the following day. Residents or guests at the Clock House, of course, had to make their way along the Dunmow Causeway before they could join the diligence, necessitating a cold and early start. Another slightly uncertain link with the capital was Stubbing's van, which came in every Saturday from a village three miles away, picked up meat from the weekly market, delivered it in Whitechapel, and returned on Mondays. Between these incursions from the outer world, Dunmow drowsed contentedly between its two annual fairs in May and November. If roadmenders ever disturbed it, their habits seemed little different from those of today. Writing to a friend in 1791, Cowper describes his own local roads as 'in a chaotic condition':

About three weeks since they dug up the street, and having done so, left it. But it will not continue long in such disorder. . . . Already they have filled up two abominable ponds, more foetid than human nostrils could endure; they were to be found, as you must remember, one just under Farmer Archer's window, and the other a little beyond it. Covered drains are to be made wherever covered drains are wanted, and the causey is to be new laid.

Dunmow 'causey' could have done with similar inprovement, but seems not to have had it.

So Sir George grew up in the rural quiet of Essex while a hundred and fifty miles away, over a very uncertain system of roads, his Coleorton inheritance smouldered peacefully among 'the beautiful pastures of this little verdant county of Leicester', as Cobbett approvingly described it. Indeed it literally smouldered, for most of its inhabitants made their living in or from the coalmines among which it stood. Surface coal had been mined there since Tudor times, and fires could easily be ignited by any carelessness. Burton reported that in Henry VIII's time the coalmines 'did burne many years together, and could not be quenched, untill that sulphurous and brimstony matter (whereupon it wrought) was utterly exhausted and consumed'. Out of the two hundred and twenty seven inhabitated houses of Coleorton in 1801, only eighty-eight persons were engaged in agriculture. Nearly all others worked in some way in the coal fields, apart from the six farmers who had their own wagons, the three hosiers 'who comb their wool and convert it into stockings', and three master hat makers. (The demand for millinery seems to have been surprisingly high if we are to judge by this! – though it perhaps includes those delightful straw hats once worn by horses in the heat of summer.) Despite all this, the natural beauty of the woods and fields was little spoiled, for the coal fields were small, and the village was modestly prosperous. Nichols' *History of Leicestershire*, in 1795, reported that most of the people had a decent house built by their parents or themselves, 'with a garden to each from an acre to an acre and a half, taken out of the common; paying 20s. an acre for the land, and a small ackowledgment for the house, to the lords of the soil'.

Sir George's predecessors were good landlords. The last Viscount Beaumont had founded a hospital for six poor widows, each having a separate house and garden, the houses all contained within a single pleasant brick building; while above the whole was a free school for reading and writing, 'considerable and in good reputation'. A Beaumont charity provided gowns for the widows and coal for them and the schoolmaster. To Sir George's mother all must have seemed well enough, and she probably took little interest in the Leicestershire property. Dunmow was her own home and that of her family, and there she kept her son until he was old enough for Eton.

CHAPTER II

Education of a Future Patron

Sir George Beaumont entered Eton at the tender age of 11 in 1764. Public schools were then so harsh that at many of them open rebellions flared among the pupils, but Eton at this time was rising in reputation owing to the wise and able rule of Edward Barnard, who was then Headmaster. Unfortunately he retired in the year after young Sir George was admitted, and was succeeded by a lesser man, John Foster, under whom the numbers dropped again; and there was even another quite serious rebellion just before Sir George left, in which many of the boys marched off to Maidenhead. It is unlikely that he took part in this himself, as he was an Oppidan and enjoyed the extra licence of those who lived in lodgings in the town. He seems in any case to have been reasonably happy at school. A near neighbour from Essex went up with him – Charles Maynard, who was later to succeed his cousin as 2nd Viscount Maynard of Easton, the estate which bordered the Howlands' Stonehall property in Dunmow. Two younger Maynard brothers soon followed; and in 1768 came Henry Phipps, who was to become a close and lifelong friend. Perhaps in his kindness he protected the youngster as he did others, although in the adult world Phipps proved much more fitted than Sir George for the rough and tumble of public life. As the 3rd Baron Mulgrave he was to have a distinguished career as Chancellor of the Duchy of Lancaster, then Secretary for Foreign Affairs in the critical period of 1805–6, then as First Lord of the Admiralty and later Master-General of the Ordnance. He was created Earl of Mulgrave in 1812, just a month before Sir George erected his cenotaph to Reynolds. (Sir George had then been urging him to give up 'the contentions of politics' as 'irksome and injurious to the health', and to seek 'the comforts of a dignified retirement'.)

But this was still far in the future, and meanwhile the small boy straight from his quiet, comfortable, ordered home, under the homely despotism of Lady Beaumont, must have been at first bewildered by the extraordinary mixture of rigour and licence that then prevailed at Eton. The hours of study were austerely regulated, though with a less monastic severity than at Winchester. Yet there were many long periods in the week, wholly unsupervised, in which the boys could do much as they liked, and roam the neighbouring countryside at will. It was then that, as his schoolfellow Henry Angelo reports:

Sir George, though as lively as his compeers, was fond of wandering alone in the sequestered spots adjacent to the College, and doubtless there felt the charm of those poetic effects which abound at sober eve, where all is rich in those attributes of art and nature, which constitute the picture – ancient towers and turrets, woodlands, glades, and water.

The official syllabus of the school seems to us so aridly medieval that one wonders how so many Etonians achieved their later distinction. The compulsory subjects were grammar and composition, studied from a Latin grammar which was an abbreviation of that written by Lily for St Paul's School in Henry VIII's reign, the reading of Greek and Latin authors, repetitions, and the writing of themes and verses. Older boys also learned enough history and geography to provide a background for the study of classical authors. But it was in the hours not devoted to this official syllabus that an apt and intelligent boy could pick up those interests which really formed the tastes and accomplishments of the gentleman to be. He could attend short lessons in French, geography, and mathematics; the famous Italian family of Angelo kept a fencing school for those who wished to learn; swimming was a delightful occupation for warm summer afternoons. Henry

Angelo, who was himself a small boy at the school at this time, and inclined to hero-worship his elder, says that Sir George was the best swimmer in the school.

He was remarkably inclined to be fat, and consequently so buoyant, that he could, and frequently did, remain in the water for one or two hours; and having been persuaded that the frequency of bathing would reduce him in size, he for one period might be said to be amphibious, living almost as much in as out of that element.

Looking at the elegant portraits of the grown Sir George it is hard to think of him as one of the fat boys of the school; although one wonders whether the 'low fevers' of which he so often complained in later life may have had their origin in these unduly long periods of exposure. But his passion for the water never left him; and he once told the story of how, when abroad, he had tried to swim to the bottom of a very deep, clear lake. He secured a stone to a line which he twisted loosely round his left arm before diving in. He kept his eyes open under water as he sank until, suddenly slipping into blackness, he had the sense to untwist the line and shoot upwards. Even so he was nearly exhausted by the time he surfaced, and England had nearly lost her National Gallery even before the project could be conceived.

Boys in the upper school were also expected to become conversant with Shakespeare, Milton, Addison, and Pope. Such study was all the more fruitful because pursued in greater freedom; a master who read well and was himself an enthusiast might hope to give his scholars a lasting love of the best of English writing. Sir George came to it with a natural readiness. He had already the quick responsiveness to beauty in any form, the liveliness of mind, which were characteristic of his adult life. He fell early in love with Shakespeare, and is said to have known whole plays by heart before he left school. He had considerable histrionic gifts, which he loved to exercise even into his old age, and he was to be the friend of many professional actors. His friend Henry Phipps caught some of his enthusiasm, and persuaded his family and friends to help him produce Otway's *Venice Preserved* during the Christmas vacation. But this was a very youthful and highly respectable performance, with none of the dubious opportunities so regrettably exploited by some of the young persons in *Mansfield Park*.

But the greatest thing which Eton ever did for the future 'first of modern amateur painters, and very friendly patron of certain professors of their art', was to bring him under the tutorship of the drawing master, Alexander Cozens. Cozens was a gifted and fashionable teacher, who had taught drawing to the Prince of Wales, as well as an able artist: a certain romance attached to him also on the report, now thought erroneous, that he was a natural son of Peter the Great of Russia. Young Beaumont was considered his most promising pupil at the time, and he learned a great deal despite the liveliness of the lessons, as described by Henry Angelo:

The two best scholars were the late Lord Maynard for horses, Sir George for landscapes. Though I was then a little boy, he took notice of me, ever placing me by his side at the drawing table; and many an evening have I neglected those lessons from which I might have benefited, in order to amuse ourselves in pelting bread at each other, instead of using it for our designs. Sir George, when that amusement prevailed, took me under his protection, the little ones generally receiving the brunt of the action, boy-like taking an advantage of their master, who was a little man, remarkably good-natured, and mild in his manners. The drawing room, which was at Cole's, the village barber, was a famous winter inducement to learn to draw, where noise and fun too often supplied the place of the pencil.

Cozens may have been no disciplinarian, but he was attentive and painstaking with those who wished to learn. He had his own method, adapted from Leonardo's hint that he was often inspired by the irregular patches of damp appearing on the plaster walls of his room. Cozens would float smudges and blots in black, brown, or grey, on to damp paper which, 'with a certain degree of ingenious coaxing, he converted into romantic rocks, woods, towers, steeples, cottages, rivers, fields, and waterfalls'. Sometimes he made his blots on the underside of earthenware plates, which were then pressed on to the paper. Such methods, together with the *joie de vivre* of his lively classes, resulted in masses of spoiled paper, and bitter complaints from the 'dame' of the mess made at the evening meal when the young gentlemen used the same plates with which they had been making their smudges. Most of them were indeed 'incorrigible blotters'; but Cozens recognized Sir George's natural aptitude, aroused his enthusiasm, and encouraged and guided his taste. Before he left Eton the boy was already a keen amateur of the arts.

During these years at Eton an event happened at home that was to alter the quiet pattern of Sir George's life at Dunmow. When he was fifteen, his mother married for the second time. Oddly enough, among all the letters of his circle, the diaries, the memoirs and notices which still survive, there seems not a single reference to this event. The only trace is in the parish register of Great Dunmow, which records the marriage by special licence, on August 15, 1768, of John Gates, widower of the parish of Dedham, to Rachel Beaumont of the parish of Great Dunmow, witnessed by Mrs Patrick and Joanna Howland – the oldest and youngest sisters of the bride. This union lasted for twenty-one years, yet the evidence is so slight that one wonders whether the fifty-year-old dowager committed a social indiscretion in marrying a little beneath her, which her family preferred to ignore as far as possible in a well-bred silence; the romances of middle age are in any case inexplicable to the children. The unknown Mr Gates has left only the most elusive shadow behind him. Local records reveal no trace, with the single exception of the land tax assessments for the Hundred of Dedham, but these certainly suggest that there was a difference of fortune between John Gates and his second wife, if not a difference of rank. Until June 14, 1787, John Gates was paying land tax on property rated at £26 10 0, and then his name disappears altogether. But for the next nine years Lady Beaumont (under the name of her first marriage) paid tax on a property which she rented from one John Freeman, with a rateable value of £77 10 0, while herself letting a smaller property to an Arthur Hemming. One infers the death of John Gates in 1787, and his widow's subsequent removal to a larger house more befitting the relict of a Beaumont than the relict of a Gates. Then in 1797 her name as a tenant of John Freeman also disappears, although she was still letting her own property to Hemming. It was presumably in this year that she returned to her old home at Dunmow as a dower house, where we know her to have lived for the rest of her long life.

No one can now know the effect of this rather odd and unexpected marriage upon Lady Beaumont's son. Certainly it caused no rift between them, for Sir George always spoke of his mother with the warmest affection and respect, and he stayed a number of times in her house at Dedham – though there is still no mention of John Gates' existence. He is ignored even in the final record of the woman who was once Rachel Howland, inscribed on a tablet on the north wall of Dunmow parish church:

In this chancel are deposited
the remains of
Sir George Beaumont Bart
of this place
who died February IV. MDCCLXII
aged XXXVI years
and of
Dame Rachel his wife
who died May V. MDCCCXIV
aged XCVI years

The dreaded hour is come, tis come, tis past!
That gentle sigh, dear mother, was the last:
And now diffus'd among the blest above
Glows the pure spirit of maternal love:

Ting'd by whose beams my very failings shone
Grac'd in thy eyes with something not their own.
No more affection shall thy fancy cheat,
Or warp thy judgment when again we meet,
But every action in its native hue
Rise undisguis'd and open to thy view.
May every action then be duly weigh'd,
Each virtue cherish'd and each duty paid,
That when my trembling soul shall wing her flight
Thro' death's dark valley to the realms of light,
I may expect where no false views beguile
The approving look and that accustom'd smile,
Blest smile! becoming her sublime abode,
And harbinger of pardon from my God.

Erected to the memory of his parents by
Sir George Howland Beaumont Bart
of Coleorton Hall
in the county of Leicester.

There is something here more warm and genuine than a merely conventional tribute, despite the accustomed jog-trot of sepulchral verse. But there may well have been some initial strain or time of adjustment, possibly reflected in the last year before Sir George went up to Oxford, which he passed almost entirely in the company of his tutor, the Rev Mr Davy.

It was in the spring of this year, and in Mr Davy's company, that he paid a visit which was to give new direction and impetus to his youthful enthusiasm. During a stay in London the tutor took his young pupil to call upon William Woollett. The artist had achieved distinction early in his career, and was at this time engraver to the king. An article in the *Gentleman's Magazine* a few years later attributes largely to Woollett a change in the balance of trade in prints. During the eighteenth century England had imported large numbers of prints from Italy, France, and Holland; but by the end of the century we were exporting far more than we imported, up to the value of £60,000. After the romantic 'blottings'

C

learned under Alexander Cozens, Beaumont was deeply interested in the fine precision of the engraver's draughtsmanship, and not repelled by his manner, although Blake described him on one occasion as 'a heavy lump of cunning and ignorance'. Certainly he believed in self-expression, in an age which still allowed scope for personality. Although he lived in the very respectable neighbourhood of Rathbone Place, he was wont to celebrate the completion of a plate by firing off a cannon from the roof of his house. Luckily for the neighbours, the engraver's art is slow, so that such exuberance would be infrequent.

Living with Woollett at this time, and nearly at the end of a six years' apprenticeship to him, was Thomas Hearne. All his life Sir George was a man of quick enthusiasms and lasting friendships. He was at once attracted by Hearne, who was probably the first of the many artists he was always to befriend, and for whose families he showed a warm concern whenever the need arose. He delightfully recalls the youthful happiness of that first acquaintance in a letter written years later to Dr Monro:

I first became acquainted with him in the spring of 1771. I came with my tutor, Mr Davy, to London, and as my fondness for art made me desirous of seeing the most celebrated professors in every line, he carried me to his friend, Mr Woollett. We mounted up to his garret and there sat Hearne, most assiduously employed in etching from a picture by Swaneveldt, now in my possession. We passed about six weeks in London and there were few days in which we did not spend some hours in the company of Woollett and Hearne. We talked incessantly of pictures and plates, and my love for painting was completely confirmed. Mr Woollett was prevailed upon to promise a visit to Mr Davy in the course of the summer and bring Hearne with him; accordingly in August they arrived at his house at Henstead in Suffolk.

There we passed six weeks together, I may almost say, as far as I was concerned, in perfect happiness. We sketched all day and in the evening we were delighted with the original pleasantry and inimitable humour of Mr Davy. I am sure you must have heard Hearne speak of him. We visited Houghton and saw that collection with delight.

The remembrance of this happy year never fails, when I think of it, to cross my mind like a gleam of bright sunshine. I was young and ardent, and admiration – the most pleasing of sensations – I enjoyed in the highest degree. I thought Woollett and Hearne the greatest artists that ever existed, and if anyone had presumed to say that Claude or Gaspar knew half so much of the matter, I should have considered it as ignorance or prejudice. Woollett I knew, and regarded to the day of his death; he was an excellent man – it is unnecessary to praise him in his line. Since that time Hearne has risen daily in my esteem; a man of purer integrity does not exist.

Gently though Sir George may laugh at his own youth, his letter reflects that quality which all his life was to win men to him, that disinterested delight in admiration for others, 'the most pleasing of sensations'. The two artists found him an apt pupil; in his later life his drawings are much better than his paintings and one remembers that, although he was a friend of Reynolds, all his earlier contacts with artists were those that would make him more of a draughtsman than a colourist. Born as he was to rank and fortune, the responsibilities, the pleasures, and the distractions, of the polite world, Beaumont was never to be a professional painter, yet he had enough enthusiasm and talent to make him something more than the mere fashionable amateur; and certainly in this long summer in the rich Suffolk landscape, working with and learning from his older companions, he realized what was to be the chief joy of his life.

It was a joy that he carried with him when he went up to Oxford, and which probably protected him from some of the less creditable aspects of university life. Wordsworth, speaking of his own innocuous career at Cambridge, even at a later date, complains that 'the manners of the young men were very frantic and dissolute at that time, and Oxford was no better, or worse'. But Sir George clearly took no harm from the possible dissipations of undergraduate life, although he was lively enough and his sense of humour extended to practical jokes. On one occasion, according to Northcote, he advertised in the papers that a German artist had discovered a remarkable new method of taking an exact likeness by causing the sitter to look into a mirror which was heated high enough to bake the impression upon the glass. He gave the address of a perfumer's opposite his own lodgings in Bond Street, and amused himself next day by watching the number of credulous people who called hopefully at the shop. At length he strolled over himself, to be driven out again by an exasperated, outraged, and bewildered perfumer. And on another occasion, going with a party of gay young men to dine at a tavern, Sir George teased the waiter with the heartless cheerfulness of a Prince Hal. As the poor man waited at the coach door to hold a light, those who got out first slipped round in the flickering shadow and re-entered the vehicle from the far side – until the waiter, terrified by the endless procession of young men who could emerge from a single carriage, at last dropped his light and fled back into the tavern.

But sociable and frolicsome as he could be, Sir George still found his chief pleasure in the quiet pursuit of his own art. He was fortunate in being able to take lessons from the German drawing master, John Baptiste Malchair, who had recently settled in Oxford. From him he learned to see not only the nobility of nature, that commonplace of contemporary aestheticism, but also the *simplicity* of natural forms. He learned to use ordinary, familiar objects as the basis of a pictorial composition; and in doing so he prepared his mind for that appreciation of the ordinary, that vision of 'familiar objects as if they were not familiar' that he was to recognize in the poetry of Wordsworth, and at last in the art of Constable. If he learned nothing else than what Malchair was able to teach him, his time at Oxford was certainly not wasted.

CHAPTER III

Emergence of a Man of Fashion

The young man who came down from Oxford was not likely to find a niche in the political world, like his friend Henry Phipps; his disposition was too gentle and sensitive to relish it. But he had a real, if limited, artistic talent, a lively, pleasant, and sociable nature, and sufficient common-sense to protect him from arrogance, pomposity, or the absurdities of the professed connoisseur. His love of art was solidly based and therefore without pretension. He already numbered Reynolds and Richard Wilson among his friends, and derived from them his preference for Old Masters and the Italianate style of painting. But although he had as yet no wider experience to modify his total acceptance of their views, his love was genuine and not imitative – not a rich man's hobby, but already the ruling passion of his life.

While still at Oxford he had made friends also with another admirer of Wilson's, a man fourteen years older than himself, but a fellow-pupil under Malchair's tuition. This was Oldfield Bowles, whose boundless hospitality often included both Beaumont and Wilson; and it was under his roof that Sir George was to meet the woman who was to bring him long years of quiet happiness. His courtship there reads again like the pages from one of Jane Austen's unwritten novels.

Oldfield Bowles was one of those remarkable men whom that period sometimes bred, who gives the lie to any conception of the late Georgian country squire as a Squire Western or even a Mr Hardcastle. His estate lay in North Aston, close to the Oxfordshire, Gloucestershire, Northamptonshire borders, and included a Park Farm which he cultivated himself with such skill and enthusiasm that it was a matter of general local pride. His experiments in the breeding of sheep, mostly of the Leicestershire breed, attracted the attention even of that famous agricultural economist, Arthur Young, when he visited there on his travels through England. But this was only one of Bowles' many interests. He also maintained a botanic garden, built up a fine library, collected musical instruments and paintings, and even painted a little himself. And he also had a private theatre.

'There is always a fashionable taste,' says Peacock wickedly. 'A taste for driving the mail – a taste for acting Hamlet – a taste for philosophical lectures. . . .' Writing in 1817 he may well have had Sir George in mind, for everyone knew his perennial enthusiasm for the theatre, which was as lively in middle age as it had ever been in his youth; while in his twenties he found his friend Bowles' private stage irresistibly fascinating.

Anyone who now visits North Aston, a small village remote and dreaming in a corner of the Cotswolds, even yet undisturbed by the great main roads, must wonder wherever enough people came from to provide an audience for house-party performances. But in the 1770s it presented a very different appearance. Nothing but the accolade of a royal visit made Cheltenham the centre of fashion, rather than a near neighbour of North Aston itself – the now forgotten hamlet of Astrop. A medicinal spring had been discovered at Astrop in 1664, which soon became popular; and another was opened at King's Sutton, about a mile away, in 1749. That indefatigable traveller, Celia Fiennes, had been to Astrop a few years after the springs were discovered there, but thought little of it:

I went to Astrop where is a Steele water much frequented by the Gentry; it has some mixture of Allum so is not so strong as Tunbridge; there is a fine Gravell Walke that is between two high cutt hedges where is a Roome for the Musick and a Roome for the Company besides the Private walkes; the well runnes not very quick, they are not curious in keeping it, neither is there any bason for the spring to run out off, only a dirty well full of moss's which is all changed yellow by the water; there are lodgings about for the Company and a little place called Sutton.

Things must have inproved during the more elegant years of the eighteenth century, and the inhabitants been more 'curious' in keeping their well, for before long the two little villages had developed the gaiety and elegance of a spa.

There was a public ball at Astrop every Monday, and breakfast, cards, dancing, and an 'ordinary' for ladies and gentlemen every Friday during the season. There would be a ready-made audience of fashionable visitors whenever Oldfield Bowles wished to use his private theatre; and his father, though still alive, grew old, and was happy for his son to indulge his enthusiasms and fill the house with young people and laughter.

Certainly the local gentry were represented one summer evening when Sir George Beaumont was one of the performers. The young man was acting well, but not so far lost in his part that he was unaware of his audience. A face caught his attention – young, a little rounded, but eager and alive, and at this moment gratifyingly moved by his performance. What could be more commendable or interesting? Sir George lost no time in seeking an introduction.

His dancing star was still above him. The young lady was Margaret Willes of Astrop Manor; the families of both young people could contemplate an alliance with lively satisfaction. Sir George could offer an ancient lineage, wealth, and charm of address; the young lady's family was less noble in descent, but distinguished enough, even if a little odd. She had a pleasant face, and enough fortune to entitle her to be called a beauty. Her grandfather had been Sir John Willes, Lord Chief Justice of the Common Pleas, who had for years manoeuvred for the Woolsack with a political flexibility akin to the Vicar of Bray's and then lost it at the moment of achievement through holding out for a peerage to be conferred with it.

The office went to a less demanding candidate, and Sir John retired with his disappointment to the beautiful small manor at King's Sutton. This was the home in which Margaret Willes grew up – a square, elegantly proportioned house, in the darker kind of Cotswold stone, the colour of orchard honey rather than the paler clover honey colour of most Gloucestershire houses. She came of a long line of divines and lawyers and wealthy merchants and was bred in a tradition of Protestant piety. It was a sound heredity, though capable of odd quirks now and again. Old Sir John had his moment in the '45' when he planned a volunteer regiment of lawyers to guard the persons of the Royal family – a happy thought that was but ill received by George II. And there had been Margaret's Aunt Jane, who at twenty-two made a romantic runaway match with a young soldier – even though he later became a K.C.B. and Commander-in-Chief in India, which made it quite respectable. There was evidently a lively and romantic streak in the family which may have accounted for Thomas Monkhouse's description of Margaret Beaumont in her later years as 'a good creature – sensible, though oddish'. She was the youngest of four children, a charming, intelligent young woman, in whom romantic sensibility was ready to develop at the slightest encouragement. She already delighted in poetry, and was just as ready to share Sir George's taste in art. She needed only an object for her enthusiasms to make her a natural disciple.

They were married in 1778 – a union unhappily destined to be childless, but lasting in devoted affection for the whole of its forty-nine years.

In Coleorton church at the present day are engravings of two portraits by Sir Joshua Reynolds, painted to celebrate his young friends' marriage. The originals which once hung in the Hall have now disappeared, but the two rather sedate and youthful faces seem still to have more in common with the England of Johnson than with that of Cowper, and this not only because of the artist's style. Looking at the man who is to become the friend of Wordsworth and Constable, one is struck very forcibly by the coexistence of two worlds. The coherent 'development' recorded by the literary historian is a mere figment of the imagination. Horace Walpole had begun to amuse himself with the rebuilding of Strawberry Hill, that minor temple of the new 'Gothic' taste, in the year of Beaumont's birth. But Johnson's *Dictionary* had not then been published, and Sir George was ten before Boswell was to have his first unnerving meeting with the Great Whale. Books that we now regard as landmarks of the eighteenth century were still to come – *Rasselas*, *Tristram Shandy*, *The Idler*, *The Deserted Village*. The *Reliques of Ancient English Poetry*, newly published by Bishop Percy, or Walpole's own *Castle of Otranto*, may have been part of his spare-time reading at Eton, but Chesterfield's *Letters* were still unwritten. New young men would soon desire Beaumont's patronage; but Reynolds, Gainsborough, and Wilson were the friends whom he revered. The patron lives always between two worlds, of tradition and new creation, and his function is vindicated if he can help his own generation to sympathize with the new as well as to respect the old. It is in this that Beaumont's virtue lay. His enthusiasm, and his courteous and happy readiness to admire other men's talents, gave him the intellectual flexibility to enjoy both worlds; and through his wealth of friends among those who still led fashions in taste as well as in dress and manners he was able to make the new men acceptable. He could present experiment, as indeed he saw it, as developing rather than flouting tradition.

There is a certain suppleness of taste even in his choice of scenery, at a time when this too was to some extent governed by fashion. He loved the gentle Essex countryside as much as the more 'romantic' woods of Coleorton; but he had also fallen under the spell of Cumberland twenty years or so before it became the elegant thing to tour the English Lakes if one could not afford the Grand Tour of the Continent. So he took his bride for a long honeymoon residence at Keswick, though perhaps also visiting the cottage on Loughrigg Tarn which he loved so well that he at one time thought of building a house in the neighbourhood. While there he once again met Thomas Hearne, who was staying nearby with Joseph Farington. From time to time, for many years, he was to go on a painting tour with one or other of these artists; but where Farington remained always somewhat on the periphery of his circle, Hearne had some part of his heart. They shared a love of the mountains and the stillness, the wind and cloud of Cumberland. For both it was a painter's country. a place to which the Beaumonts were to return again and again. Yet still, by tradition and fashion, the real painter's country was Italy; and so in October 1781 the young pair set out for the Continent, Sir George rather belatedly making the Grand Tour which properly completed a gentleman's education.

Despite the chill which he caught on the channel crossing, and the tedious discomforts of travel, even in the convenience of one's own coach brought over from England, Sir George's first meeting with Italy was a case of love at first sight, just as his first experience of the Lakes had been. Its light and colour were an ever-recurring miracle to him. He writes delightedly in his old age, as freshly as he might have done on this first visit, 'there is enough ultramarine in this sky to pay the national debt'. He went prepared to admire, to gaze upon scenes of sublimity and grandeur, to stand in reverence before the world's greatest pictures, hitherto known to him only through engravings. For any intelligent young man the Grand Tour must have been a voyage of discovery; but for one for whom both the enjoyment and practice of art were a passion, it had a peculiarly rich satisfaction. To see those places where Raphael himself had painted, to gaze, lost in romantic reflection, upon the house where Claude had lived, to wander in the great galleries and paint in the Italian sunshine – and all in the company of a young and charming wife – this was indeed to fall in love again.

While on this tour he met, apparently for the first time, the son of his old drawing master at Eton. John Robert Cozens was acting as travelling companion to that very eccentric but very wealthy young man, William Beckford, who had just completed his Arabian romance of *Vathek*. *Vathek* caught the public fancy, with the increasingly improbable adventures of its megalomaniac hero, who meets his deservedly evil end at last in the infernal halls of Eblis. This was an aspect of romanticism which Sir George could never take seriously – Byronic melodrama was not suited to his temperament; but the author, who had tried in this curious form to exorcise some inward experience of his own, was in a state of feverish sensibility of which this spell of foreign travel was intended to cure him. Cozens must have found Beaumont's cheerful sociability, his nice sense of balance, a restful change from the nervous excitability of his charge: while Beaumont was already sufficiently a connoisseur to recognize in the other a new and original talent, a poetry of vision which was to give a new direction to English topographical art. Cozens's place in the artistic history of his period belongs to a later chapter, but his company at this time was to help Sir George himself to develop still further as a landscape painter.

It was 1784 before the Beaumonts returned to England; but they were still unready to settle either to the life of London fashion or to country retirement. They lived chiefly in the London house at the corner of Grosvenor Square. But in the next four or five years Sir George found time for sketching tours of the Lakes, the West Country, and Wales – sometimes in the company of Hearne or Farington – as well as for long visits to his mother at Dedham. The Leicestershire estates were little thought of, although he was sufficiently uneasy about Joseph Boultbee, the son of his father's steward at Coleorton, to refuse to renew his lease of various properties.

Perhaps he was irked by a nagging sense of duty, for one other experience was generally expected of him. He had acquired the education and tastes of a gentleman, he had taken a wife as became the owner of estates, but he had not yet taken any part in public life. Probably he guessed, even before trying it, that he would find it distasteful; but in 1790 he did as his mother, his tenants, and his friends expected of him, and allowed himself to be returned to Parliament as one of the two members for Beer Alston in Devon. At least he was spared the trouble, extra expense, and distasteful rowdyism of a contested election, for his seat could be bought – for a pretty large consideration – through the goodwill of its owner. Beer Alston is described by Oldfield in his *Representative History of Great Britain and Ireland* (1816) as a hamlet near Tavistock owned by the Earl of Beverly, having about forty cottages 'of the meanest and most miserable description'. The right of election was in the freehold tenants, holding by burgage tenure, and paying 3d. per annum to the lord of the borough. The number of electors depended upon the earl himself, who followed the common practice of filling his cottages with suitable persons who lived in them – for a con- sideration – until the election was over, and then resigned their burgage tenures to the owner again. There were some- times as many as a hundred tenures though, as Oldfield grimly remarks, 'the number of voters may be said to be efficiently but one'. By this system everyone was kept happy – the electors who were able to sell their votes, the owner who made a handsome profit out of the whole affair, and the mem- ber who obtained his seat with no trouble other than expense. Generally it was thought to work out well enough: a landed gentleman with sufficient sense of responsibility might be trusted to do his honest best for the country, however he got his seat. The only people who complained were the inhabitants of those great industrial towns who had no representative at all; but who could expect a mob of grimy-handed machine minders to know what was really best for them in the long run? The Society of the Friends of the People, and the London Corresponding Society, founded to promote Par- liamentary reform, show that the social conscience of England was beginning to awake to the scandal of the rotten borough:

[44]

but it would be harsh to complain of the acquiescence of this rather half-hearted new recruit when so many greater men still found nothing abhorrent in the system. Indeed his more powerful friend, Lord Lonsdale, was still using the *force majeure* of a local despot as late as 1816. When Brougham dared to seek election in the Lowther's own constituency of Cumberland, the Earl brought sailors and carpenters from Liverpool at a fee of five shillings a day, with two hundred special constables in arms to 'keep the peace' at the polling booths! But Sir George, like many another worthy gentleman, was returned in a manner generally acceptable, and with the best intentions in the world. He succeeded a much more famous member than himself, for the constituency had previously been represented by the Marquis of Wellesley; but the latter's administration offended Beverley, who refused his re-election.

For one of his temperament, poor Sir George could hardly have chosen a more unhappy time to represent his country. His politics, such as they were, were a matter of inherited prejudices rather than intellectual conviction, and his heart was not in them. This was the year after the fall of the Bastille, in which feelings and fears ran high, whether one dreaded the outbreak of anarchy or felt a new impetus given to the cause of reform. Many younger men were still hailing the outbreak of the French revolution as the dawn of a new and more enlightened age, divining in its first phases only a more drastic and more drastically needed kind of reform movement, akin to that already afoot in England. But one could hardly expect a Beaumont to see eye to eye with them. Sir George came of a class which for generations had accepted the tasks of government both as its right and its duty. He was no quicker than many other well-intentioned and inexperienced politicians to see when the Parliamentary machine had ceased to correspond with the needs of the nation, while an alarming personal experience that year was hardly likely to increase his confidence in the spread of democracy. He had gone over to Paris on a brief visit that summer, far more interested in art than in politics, and delighted to make the acquaintance of the French painter, David, while he was there. The coming and going of Englishmen in Paris, the as yet untroubled existence of its little English community, show clearly that the situation was still regarded by many people as a matter of internal and almost local politics. Englishmen imagined they had little to fear in France. Those of a reforming spirit felt themselves most happily to be welcomed as apostles from a freer and more enlightened nation, and many of them delighted in the spirit of the times. Young Mr Wordsworth, for instance, who also happened to be over on a university vacation, saw with enthusiasm

> *France standing on the top of golden hours,*
> *And human nature seeming born again.*

But Mr Wordsworth was at this time very much a democrat and would rather have disapproved of Sir George's existence had he been much aware of it. And the little episode which now occurred nearly deprived him of the acquaintanceship for ever.

Sir George was walking quietly through the streets of Paris, enjoying the company of his new political patron, Lord Beverley – men of consequence, accustomed to walk in safety even in this unpredictable city, and happily convinced that the French would at last come to their senses. They were destined to sudden and alarming disillusion. They turned a corner of the street straight upon a scene of hideous violence. Amid shouts of 'à la lanterne, à la lanterne', a Frenchman was being dragged savagely away, caught in one of the sudden sporadic out-bursts of mob violence. Taken by surprise, the English milords made no attempt to disguise their horror and indignation, which was like enough to make them fellow victims: but by sheer good fortune a passer-by, seeing their danger, snatched a tricolour from one of the revolutionaries and thrust it into their hats, hurrying them out of the way while he huzza'd as heartily as the rest.

It was not the kind of incident to increase an aristocrat's trust in the people. It added to the fear of anarchy which troubled many hearts in the uneasy years then and to come, as reports came in here and there of riots and violence even in England itself as men despaired for bread. Inevitably Beaumont supported Pitt and his repressive measures as a safeguard of the public interest. He and his kind were neither heartless nor stupid; they knew that the great industrial towns were virtually unrepresented; they knew that changing social conditions were bringing unprecedented poverty and hunger. No democrats deplored it more than they did, for many of them, like Sir George himself, were men who cared greatly for their own small communities, excellent landlords, ready and anxious to relieve every individual case of want as far as their power allowed. But they lacked the vision to see that the machine of government was obsolescent and needed an entire replacement; they hoped to keep it in running order by tinkering with the engine, and were convinced that drastic change spelled mortal danger. So we find Sir George supporting Pitt's Sedition Bill while regretfully telling Farington that it was a strong measure but he believed it to be necessary. He must at least have felt sustained by the scandalized protest of the inhabitants of his own Dunmow, alarmed and indignant at the spread of the corresponding societies and their campaign for electoral reform. The little paper-covered notebook containing the Great Dunmow Overseers Accompt gives the minutes of an unusual parish meeting, under the impressive heading of 'Resolutions and Declarations':

At a Meeting of the Inhabitants of the Hundred of Dunmow, and several Adjoining parishes, in the County of Essex holden at the Saracens head in Great Dunmow on Tuesday the first day of January 1793.

Whereas certain publications, at once inconsistent with the

fundamental principles of the English Government, Subversive of Civil subordination, destructive of social happiness; and by their fallacious plausibility, strongly tending to excite Sedition, have been dispersed among the people of this kingdom; and an opinion generally prevails that Associations have been formed, and Correspondences entered into calculated to Introduce Confusion and anarchy.

We, inhabitants of the Hundred of Dunmow, and Adjoining parishes, think it our Duty to Declare our zealous attachment to the British Constitution; consisting of King; Lords and Commons, our full Conviction of the advantages derived from it to persons of all Ranks, and all denominations, and our firm Confidence that as it has Attained its present degree of perfection by successive improvements through a long Series of Ages, so it is fully competent to make such further Improvements, as from time to time may be found expedient.

And we therefore Resolve that we will oppose to the utmost of our power all Attempts to Subvert, Injure or Disparage it, and use our best endeavours to bring to justice all such persons as shall utter treasonable words; post up; or Distribute inflammatory handbills; or Adopt any other Means to Raise Commotions, Excite Disloyalty to the King or Disaffection to the Government.

And in Order that the zeal of no person may carry him beyond proper bounds, we Declare that we will Exert our utmost endeavours to prevent every Insult or Protestation to individuals, which may at any time take place, to the terror or injury of his Majesty's loyal and peaceable subjects.

And it is recommended to the Officers of the said parishes and hamlets, within the Hundred of Dunmow to transcribe the said resolution and Declarations and to request a Signature of Approbation of them; from all such principal Inhabitants of their Respective parishes, that may not have Attended this Meeting that their such Signatures and now obtained be entred with these resolutions and Declarations in the parish book in which the Overseers Accounts are usually kept and that they be brought for the Inspection of the Magistrates at their next Meeting that thus the Whole may Remain a perpetual memorial of the Attachment of the Hundred of Dunmow to the principles of the British Constitution and be Satisfactory Evidence that it is not the Language of party, but the General Voice of the people.

Resolved Unanimously

That the Thanks of this Meeting be given to the Revd Nicholas Toke for Convening this Meeting.

Resolved Unanimously

That the Thanks of this Meeting be given to the Revd Henry Maynard, not only for his readiness in taken the Chair, and his Conduct in it, but also for his Excellent Speech, in Deffence of the British Constitution.

Resolved Unanimously

That the thanks of this Meeting be given to the Revd John Howlett, for Drawing up the above Resolutions and Declarations.

Resolved Unanimously

That the Letter presented to this Meeting by Mr Wm Johns from the protestant Dissenters within the Hundred of Dunmow and Signed by a Vast Number of Respectable persons be inserted in the Chelmsford Chronicle, the County Chronicle, and the General Evening Post.

John Parsons ⎫
John Barnard ⎬ Churchwardens

James Scruby ⎫
Wm Portway ⎬ Overseers
John Scruby ⎭

The flourish of capitals and the anarchic punctuation breathe the very zeal of the recorder; but although the next page of the notebook is left blank, no signatures appear. Sir George would most probably be in London at the time; but as young Henry Maynard, his neighbour and his junior at Eton, was there, he would certainly hear all about it.

In the two years following this agitated affair at Dunmow, the reform movement had gathered impetus. Its more responsible leaders were desperately concerned to keep it within the constitution; their aim was not revolution but a representative franchise which might lead to some real and permanent improvement of the lot of the thousands who as yet had no one to speak for them. But every local bread riot called up in many people's minds a picture of the Paris mob and the September massacres. It would take a quarter of a century to allay the apprehensions of the law-abiding, so wickedly described by Henry Tilney in *Northanger Abbey*:

My stupid sister has mistaken all your clearest expressions. You talked of expected horrors in London; and instead of instantly conceiving, as any rational creature would have done, that such words could relate only to a circulating library, she immediately pictured to herself a mob of three thousand men assembling in St George's Fields; the Bank attacked, the Tower threatened, the streets of London flowing with blood, a detachment of the 12th Light Dragoons (the hopes of the nation) called up from Northampton to quell the insurgents, and the gallant Captain Frederick Tilney, in the moment of charging at the head of his troop, knocked off his horse by a brick-bat from an upper window.

It was an unhappy time for men of moderation. Courtesy and restraint were innate in Sir George's character, not merely the mark of breeding, and he was deeply distressed by the acrimony that attended the passing of the Sedition Bill. It was the culmination of his distaste for political life. On November 24, 1795, he reported unhappily to Farington that 'the altercation was more violent and disagreeable than any he remembers. Windham is so warm, that he did and frequently does commit himself by unguarded expressions, and Fox went to such lengths as to be content [compelled?] to explain his meaning.' 'Sir George,' adds Farington, 'seems not to wish to be in another Parliament.'

He was too gentle to share his friend, Lord Mulgrave's, enjoyment of the heady dangers of crisis, of the spectacle of Pitt triumphantly riding out the storm in the following year – when, as Mulgrave wrote, he 'ought to have given anything to have been in Parliament to have heard Pitt's speech in defence of his having sent £1,200,000 to the Emperor without the consent of Parliament – to have heard him defend his head with his brains'. But Beaumont was only too thankful not to have been there. He had abandoned his seat at the close of Parliament, and must have listened with some inward irony to Nathaniel Dance's[1] boast that he had just paid £4,000 for a seat in the new one, as well as £50 laid out on a 'treat' for the electors of East Grinstead. If a new Parliament should be called in a year or two, proclaimed Dance, he 'should think himself very ill-used, if required to pay again at the end of so short a time'. Sir George could accept with equanimity the investment of the purchase money, but could not agree with the sentiment.

He was prepared to spend £80 himself on a 'treat' for Great Dunmow, but this was not to win votes but to celebrate a victory after a year of alarms. In February 1797 there had even been a small French expeditionary force which landed in Pembrokeshire, though it quickly surrendered. Lord Duncan's victory at Camperdown was all the more welcome when it came, and Sir George marked it by giving a whole ox to be roasted at Dunmow, when 'many hundreds partook of the cheer of eating and drinking'. In other ways too he enlivened his local town. He was still an addict of the theatre, and well acquainted with its actors. An advertisement of July 29, 1797, announces a theatrical performance to be presented 'by desire of Sir G. Beaumont, bart' at the Theatre, New Street, Dunmow. The programme was to include Vanbrugh's *The Provoked Husband*. This was most probably an inn or barn performance, but the reference to the site as 'the Theatre' suggests that it was used with fair frequency.

These cheerful episodes suggest that Sir George still thought of himself as the squire of Dunmow more than of Coleorton. But about this time several things combined to turn his thoughts towards his Leicestershire property. To begin with, he had just discovered the justice of his earlier suspicions about his agent there.

[1] Nathaniel Dance (1735–1811), an older brother of Sir George's architect, George Dance. Nathaniel added Holland to his name on his entry to Parliament, where he represented East Grinstead for many years. He was created Sir Nathaniel Dance-Holland, Bart, in 1800.

On the north wall of Coleorton church there is still a monument to Joseph Boultbee and his wife, erected 'by their son Joseph Boultbee in remembrance of parents eminently distinguished by their Christian lives and conversation; and by him most affectionately beloved and esteemed'. The Pecksniff family could hardly have bettered this touching and warm-hearted tribute from one rogue to another. Old Mr Boultbee had lived comfortably for many years on the profits of his dishonest stewardship, residing in his master's house and working his master's mines. He had been employed by Sir George's father who was glad enough to have a tenant to keep the deserted family mansion from decay. Three years later the agent took a twenty-one year lease of Sir George's colliery and fire engine, with a clause that he was not to take out more than 10,000 loads of coal in any one year. (One wonders by what doubtful means an under-steward had obtained enough capital for this venture.) The elder Sir George then trustingly abandoned the whole affair to the hands of his principal agent, Thomas Bridge, who continued to act for the young heir. Like his master, Joseph Boultbee also had a son with his own name, who later partnered him, and when the father died, highly respected, at the ripe age of ninety, the younger man succeeded to his position. The employer lived in another county; the principal agent had a confiding nature, limited intelligence, and little knowledge of the coal-mining industry. The Boultbees soon realized that he accepted their accounts without question or investigation, so that by various false charges, errors, and omissions, they began to cut a very respectable figure in the world. There must have been some momentary suspicion when the younger Sir George returned from his first Italian Tour, as he refused for a while to renew the lease – not that this disturbed the Boultbees, who quietly continued to work the colliery without authority and to open a new one as well. Finally they obtained a new lease, and at very favourable terms for the old colliery, which they represented as almost exhausted. In 1790 old Joseph

COLEORTON HALL, LEICESTERSHIRE. — Seat of Sir Geo. Beaumont Bart.

5. *Coleorton Hall, Leicestershire,* by William Westall

(The house as it was built for Sir George by George Dance. It has since been altered)

6. *Hagar and the Angel*, by Claude Lorrain

died in full enjoyment of his wicked stewardship, paying a tithe of the value of one mine while extracting from it even more than his original contract permitted, and using the other to juggle with his master's interests to his own advantage and that of the neighbouring landlord – no doubt on commission. One likes to think that his monument was duly erected for posterity before retribution finally caught up. The year after he left Parliament Sir George made a full investigation, turned out the younger Boultbee, and in 1798 filed a Chancery suit against him. The Lord Chancellor Loughborough, though evidently astonished that the affair had gone undiscovered for so long, found against Boultbee; and in a rehearing brought by the steward, Lord Eldon upheld his predecessor's judgment. Beaumont ultimately recovered some £13,000, although he always declared this to be only a tithe of what Boultbee really owed him.

Meanwhile the whole worrying business renewed the owner's interest in Coleorton and revived his romantic love for it. The old manor now stood empty, a dull and rather inconvenient building, with neither the romance of age nor the elegance of fashion. Yet in the very year of Boultbee's disgrace, the convenience of some seat other than Dunmow was becoming apparent. The Dowager Lady Beaumont, at the age of 83, had decided to give up the lease of her house at Dedham and return to her son's home – an arrangement which brought her back to the neighbourhood of her own family at Stonehall and within much easier reach from the London house. The Clock House must become the dower house. And just at this juncture the dowager's brother, George Howland of Haverhill, died, leaving the whole of his large estate to his nephew. Such a combination of circumstances pointed to the obvious decision. Sir George erected a grateful tablet to his uncle's memory in Dunmow church, and used part of his legacy for the rebuilding of Coleorton Hall.

Friendship as well as taste directed his choice of George Dance as his architect. They had been intimates for many years. But it was in any case an obvious choice, for the younger Dance had just been appointed as Professor of Architecture at the Royal Academy, of which he was a foundation member – though oddly enough he never lectured there, and from the time of his appointment he exhibited nothing at the Academy except portraits in chalk. As the man who had rebuilt Newgate before he was thirty, the son of the designer of the London Mansion House, St Botolph's, and Aldgate, George Dance was very much a fashionable architect.

The new house and, later, its garden, were to occupy the Beaumonts very happily for the next ten years. Dance surmised that they spent some £15,000 upon it, together with £5,000 for new furniture, a lavish sum when one considers the value of money at the time; but now that the income of the Stonehall and Haverhill estates was added to the Leicestershire property and the revenue from the coalmines, Sir George enjoyed a fortune of about £8,000 a year. He himself, as became a gifted amateur, attended chiefly to the fabric of the building, Lady Beaumont to the furnishings. George Dance complained later of her lack of taste, but this was in 1808 when too close a business relationship had caused an unfortunate strain between him and his employers, and a certain waspishness creeps into his references to them. (Soon after Coleorton was finished, Sir George recommended Smirke to Lord Lonsdale when he was thinking of rebuilding.) Yet Margaret Beaumont's wry comments upon ostentation suggest an elegant refinement of taste, and sober judgment. She remarks of the Marquis of Stafford's newly renovated house that 'the long succession of rooms, their spaciousness and loftiness had such an effect that people in them looked like Lilliputians, which produced one good effect: all awe of persons was done away for no one seemed of consequence enough to make any particular impression'; or again she deplores the Carlton House furniture which 'draws all eyes away from the guests, however fine'. There speaks the girl from the quiet Cotswold manor, the hostess to whom people matter more than houses. She reminds one of General Grosvenor's dry remark upon the vast dining-room new built a few years later by the Earl of Derby – 'Pray, are those great doors to be opened for every pat of butter that comes into the room?' The Beaumonts had a simpler taste. Their two-storey house, its rooms all related to a central domed hall and gallery, was elegant, spacious, beautifully proportioned, but quite unpretentious. Despite the estrangement from Dance, they commemorated their gratitude for his work in an inscription above the newly erected portal:

This house was erected on the site of the old house by Sir George Beaumont, Bart, and Dame Margaret his wife. The first stone was laid on August 21, 1804. It was inhabited for the first time on Friday, August 12, 1808. The architect was George Dance, R.A., who has manifested as much friendship by his attention to the execution of the work as he has shown good sense, taste and genius in the design.

The Regency found much virtue in an inscription: no other generation has so perfected and practised this particular form of the art of public tribute. Perhaps this kindly example of it appealed to the architect's better feelings, for his relationship with the Beaumonts was never entirely broken and later recovered some of its earlier friendliness.

In designing his new hall Sir George was undoubtedly planning a suitable background for his cherished collection of pictures. He had begun it almost as soon as he learned to paint, and his first purchases were those of a patron bent on encouraging the artists of his own country, quite as much as a collector proud of his Old Masters, or an investor with one eye on appreciating monetary values. The early nucleus of his collection contained works by Richard Wilson, Gilpin, Hearne, Girtin, and Dance; he was already, and always, an enthusiast for landscape. Then, with greater resources and maturing judgment, he began the small, exquisitely discriminated collection of some of Europe's greatest paintings which were one day to be his own superb gift to his country. Probably his first purchase among these was that which he treasured most – his adored Claude, now known as *Hagar and the Angel*. This perfect small picture, a dream of grace and light, went with him wherever he travelled. Gradually the house in Grosvenor Square became, as Cunningham[1] described it, 'a rich museum of books and paintings'. It was a time to make a modern collector sigh with envy. It is true that the war cut off the great Italian collections from the rest of Europe for a while. But the very uncertainty of the times caused pictures to come into the market by odd and sometimes devious ways, and some must have gone astray as Napoleon gathered into the Louvre the artistic loot of Europe. Some collectors were beginning to think of pictures in terms of financial investment but – despite an occasional fantastic sum – the modern inflation of prices had hardly begun, and even a gentleman of quite moderate means might hope to purchase at least one Old Master. Wordsworth tells of a gentleman in Hagley village who was delighted at the height of the French Revolution to think that it would give his nephew a chance 'to pick up a picture of first rate excellence'. 'A single piece,' said this gentleman, 'is enough, provided it be of a noble kind, and perfect in itself.' Happy the world in which such an ambition could be cherished and might even be realized, a world in which the twenty-three-year-old Constable could go into partnership with a friend to buy a Ruysdael for £70! Even for the Rembrandt (probably the *Jew Merchant*) which he bought from Lawrence in 1797, Sir George gave only 200 guineas. Five years later he asked Farington to negotiate for the purchase from Sir Charles Soane of Hogarth's *Rake's Progress*, for which he offered 600 guineas, but Soane refused to sell. At other times he added a Canaletto (*The Stonemason's Yard*), another Rembrandt, a Poussin, three more Claudes,

---

[1] Allan Cunningham (1791–1839), Scottish writer of poems and romances. From 1814 he was secretary to the sculptor, Chantrey, and thus knew many of the artists of whom he wrote in his *Lives of the Most Eminent British Painters*.

two Wilsons, and a Reynolds, besides the contemporary paintings which he commissioned. But the pride of the collection, which shared his heart with the Claudes, was Rubens' superb *Chateau de Steen*. This was the gift of Lady Beaumont, which she purchased in 1803 for 1,500 guineas out of a legacy that she had recently received. Brilliant with light and space it hung where the sun could touch it with an even warmer glow, the delight and inspiration of every visiting artist. Constable's letters to his wife, on a later visit to Coleorton, give us a glimpse of what such a privilege must have meant in the days before a National Gallery could extend it to all who wished:

Only think, I am now writing in a room full of Claudes (not Glovers, but real Claudes), Wilsons and Poussins.

[And again:] The Claudes, the Claudes, are all, all I can think of here.

And here too were the Girtins that Constable had copied with such excitement when he first came to London. If it is true, as Sir Charles Holmes says, that the study of Girtin changed Constable from an amateur into a painter, perhaps we owe more than we realize to Sir George Beaumont, in whose house he first saw and imitated them.

CHAPTER IV

Inheritance of Taste

'The approbation of Sir George Beaumont was indeed a reputation in itself,' said Cunningham, with elegant politeness. The professional critics already had a voice and, with the founding of the *Edinburgh Review* in 1802 and the *Quarterly Review* in 1809, were soon to outweigh the influence of the private patron while, as books grew cheaper and readers more numerous, the public itself was soon to decide its favourites; but at the turn of the century the patron was still an ambassador of art and letters, a channel of taste from the original genius to the public accustomed to established modes.

A good patron requires a touch of genius himself, which is why so few are distinguished among the many who buy pictures or assist writers. He needs the gift to perceive original power, to look at the unfamiliar without any barrier of resentment, above all to have humility enough to learn from those who in a material sense depend upon him. This both the Beaumonts had in full measure. Even Northcote[1] grumblingly admitted that although Sir George had 'a full sense of his claim to family distinction', he was 'very humble in other respects, in pretensions of the mind'. He needed such a gift if he was to recognize new talent, for he was born into a world of firmly established traditional values, and was in his forties before he encountered any serious challenge to the fortress of accepted ideas. He was brought up in the mental world of his early friend, Sir Joshua Reynolds, when 'taste' – as Burke had defined it – was the sum of educated habits of mind.

---

[1] James Northcote, R.A. (1746–1831), portrait and historical painter, known for his caustic conversation expressed in a strong Devonian accent.

Critical Taste does not depend upon a superior principle in men, but upon superior knowledge. . . . It is partly made up of a perception of the primary pleasures of sense, of the secondary pleasures of the imagination, and of the conclusions of the reasoning faculty.

Sir Joshua Reynolds assumed this eminently sensible pronouncement of Burke's as the basis of his own *Discourses*, which charted the aesthetics of a century, and had such authority that they were still received with respect by Wordsworth half a century later. Reynolds' whole theory of art is social, and he derives his concept of the imagination almost verbally from Burke's *Philosophical Enquiry Into the Origin of our Ideas of the Sublime and the Beautiful* (1756). He assumes serenely that

the internal fabric of our minds, as well as the external form of our bodies, being nearly uniform . . . the imagination is incapable of producing anything originally of itself, and can only vary and combine those ideas with which it is furnished by means of the senses.

Genius is the product of natural sensibility working with close attention upon the objects of sense and the existing achievements of art, storing them in the memory, and finding fresh combinations from these materials, which are common to every man who cares to study them.

Invention, strictly speaking, is little more than a new combination of those images which have been previously gathered and deposited in the memory: nothing can come of nothing: he who has laid up no materials can produce no combinations.

An erratic genius, a highly personal vision to be understood only by an enlightened few, are outside the comprehension of Sir Joshua's world. A work of art is rightly brought to the bar of common judgment, where every man has a voice because every man has access to the same materials. The chief function of the imagination is a satisfying synthesis of the common stock of ideas and experiences.

The materials of art are common but not commonplace. The artist and writer should inspire feeling by heroic vision, by sympathy with the sublime; and everybody knows quite confidently what the sublime *is*, because of Mr Burke's very useful analysis. Sublime objects induce some degree of awe or terror, causing astonishment, 'that state of the soul, in which all its motions are suspended, with some degree of horror'. (A verbal echo sounds in *Tintern Abbey*, a full generation later.)[1] It suggests infinity, which is why 'a rotund' in building or plantation has a more noble effect than the boundaries imposed by straight lines, and why in nature, poetry, or painting, 'dark, confused, uncertain images have a greater power on the fancy to form the grander passions than those have which are more clear and determinate'. The 'grander passions' are those which art should properly seek to move, and Reynolds claims that these are less stirred by objects in themselves than by the ideas associated with them.

Architecture certainly possesses many principles in common with Poetry and Painting. Among those which may be reckoned as the first is that of affecting the imagination by means of association of ideas. Thus, for instance, as we have naturally a veneration for antiquity, what ever building brings to our remembrance ancient customs and manners, such as the castles of the Barons of ancient Chivalry, is sure to give this delight. Hence it is that *towers and battlements* are so often selected by the Painter and the Poet to make a part of the composition of their ideal Landscape.

As ideas are to be the painter's material as much as the poet's, eighteenth-century art is literary in conception and often episodic in subject. Literal truth to nature matters far less than the stirring of sublime sensations, and the Italian Masters

---

[1] *Until, the breath of this corporeal frame*
And even the motion of our human blood
Almost suspended, we are laid asleep
In body, and become a living soul.

The transfer of the image is just that which would occur in a passage unconsciously remembered.

7. *Landscape*, by Sir George Beaumont

8. *The Bard*, by John Martin

9. *Phaeton in a Storm*, by J. C. Ibbetson

are therefore far more highly rated than the Dutch. Reynolds devotes a paper in the *Idler* (No. 79) to the difference between them.

The Italian attends only to the invariable, the great and general ideas which are fixed and inherent in universal Nature; the Dutch, on the contrary, to literal truth and a minute exactness in the detail, as I may say, of Nature modified by accident. The attention to these petty peculiarities is the very cause of this naturalness so much admired in the Dutch pictures, which, if we suppose it to be a beauty, is certainly of a lower order, which ought to give place to beauty of a superior kind, since one cannot be obtained but by departing from the other. . . . In Painting, as in Poetry, the highest style has the least of common nature.

There is a comfortable solidity about the *Discourses*. Reynolds knew precisely whom one should admire, and why. Armed with a knowledge of them and of Burke's *Philosophical Enquiry*, a gentleman could hardly go wrong. One placed Raphael above all others, because of his serene and flawless presentation of ideal form. The tumultuous energy of Michelangelo is rather too disturbing; he is the 'Homer' of painting, epic indeed, yet a little primitive, although Reynolds himself in his later years begins to yield him the palm. Salvator Rosa, Titian, and Poussin are in the true heroic mould. As to landscape, Claude is the true idol, though others earn an honourable mention; and Sir Joshua bequeathes his own Sebastian Bourdon to Beaumont as a safe model of the art. No one in Europe would have disputed a word of Reynolds' doctrine. The French art historian, Roger de Piles, had already defined the essence of 'heroick landskips'.

The heroick style is a composition of objects, which, in their kinds, draw, both from art and nature, everything that is great and extraordinary in either. The situations are perfectly agreeable and surprising. The only buildings are temples, pyramids, ancient places of burial, altars consecrated to the divinities, pleasure-houses of regular architecture: And if nature appear not there, as we every day casually see her, she is at least represented as we think she ought to be. The style is an agreeable illusion, and a sort of enchantment, when handled by a man of fine genius.

So reasonable, so lucid, so comfortably familiar was the authority of Reynolds that it carried weight even with a much younger generation. When Hazlitt turns art critic he describes Nicholas Poussin's *Orion*, exhibited at the British Gallery in 1821, in terms which stress literary and associative more than visual qualities.

He applies nature to his purposes, works out her images according to the standard of his thoughts, embodies high fictions; and the first conception being given, all the rest seems to grow out of, and be assimilated to it, by the unfailing process of a studious imagination. . . . He who can show the world in its first naked glory, with the hues of fancy spread over it, or in its high and palmy state, with the gravity of history stamped on the proud monuments of vanished empire – who, by his 'so potent art', can recall time past, transport us to distant places, and join the regions of imagination (a new conquest) to those of reality – who shows us not only what nature is, but what she has been, and is capable of – he who does this, and does it with simplicity, with truth, and grandeur, is lord of nature and her powers, and his mind is universal, and his art the master-art!

In such a climate of thought, the most successful modern painters were those who came nearest to the ideal of sublimity. Richard Wilson,[1] though comparatively neglected by his immediate comtemporaries, became the doyen of the succeeding generation. Beaumont, when young, ranked him only lower than the adored and exquisite Claude. His dramatic and Italianate style – whether the actual scene were Italian or English – the romantic temples or aquaducts which fired the fancy, the golden light which so often infused the landscape as

[1] Richard Wilson, R.A. (1714–82), landscape painter. He was one of the first Academicians created by the King at the institution of the Royal Academy in 1768.

if from another and more ancient world, these were the true sublime.

The poetry of Sir George Beaumont's youth accepted the same criteria. Recognition of the familiar, however exquisite, was a minor achievement compared with the stirrings of the sublime. Mr Thomas Gray, the new poet of Sir George's Eton days, turned naturally to the ode for his more exalted moments — and nearly all his moments were exalted. His evocation of *The Bard* thrilled the young enthusiasts of his day, with its hero declaiming ruin to the ruthless king, Edward I,

As down the steep of Snowden's shaggy side
He wound with toilsome march his long array.

The wild-eyed figure 'robed in the sable garb of woe', accompanied by the ghosts of his murdered peers, and with a famished eagle screaming overhead, cried out for an artist worthy of the theme. It found one in John Martin, whose picture of *The Bard* is the very apotheosis of sublimity. Edward's troop, dwarfed by the foaming river, the towering crags, and range upon range of jagged mountains, is almost indiscernible upon one side of the torrent. On the other the bard, brandishing his harp, keeps a precarious balance on the very edge of a dark and beetling crag, while the eagle hurtles overhead. Had Gray lived to see the picture hung in the Royal Academy's exhibition of 1817 he would thoroughly have approved it.

Perhaps the eighteenth-century theory of the imagination is most aptly summed up in a picture by Julius Caesar Ibbetson and the irreverent 'sublimity' of a sixteen-year-old girl who can hardly have seen his painting, though one wonders whether an engraving of it had come her way. Ibbetson's picture, *A Phaeton in a Thunderstorm*, shows a gentleman's carriage dwarfed by towering mountains which surround the narrow road and the precipice below it, a lurid sky, bolting horses, and every sign of imminent disaster. Jane Austen, trying her fledgling wings in *Love and Freindship*, describes the final tragic downfall of Edward and the beautiful Augustus on the turnpike road.

We instantly quitted our seats and ran to the rescue of those who but a few moments before had been in so elevated a situation as a fashionably high Phaeton, but who were now laid low and sprawling in the Dust. 'What an ample subject for reflection on the uncertain Enjoyments of this World, would not this Phaeton and the Life of Cardinal Wolsey afford a thinking Mind!' said I to Sophia as we were hastening to the field of Action.

What in Gray's poem or Ibbetson's picture could exceed the final sublimity of the expiring Edward's words:

'Laura (said he, fixing his now languid Eyes on me), I fear I have been overturned.'

CHAPTER V

Portrait of a Patron

Such was the world of taste which Sir George Beaumont took for granted when he entered upon the happiest and most fruitful period of his life, freed at last from public duty – even though the dangers of the times provoked him to an occasional patriotic gesture, such as the raising of a troop of Dunmow yeomanry in 1803. One wonders how active a part this pleasant dilettante could have played, hating field sports as he did and rather bored by country squires. But Essex was near enough to France to make Coleridge uneasy for his friend's safety during the threat of invasion and to make him wish that Sir George were in Leicestershire, 'raising and organizing his Tenantry and Colliers'. Perhaps from his own brief and disastrous career as a trooper Coleridge was particularly sensitive to the dangers besetting an amateur in military affairs.

But apart from these brief alarms Beaumont managed quite successfully to forget all public anxieties in his whole-hearted pursuit of his great passion. Painting had become his life. 'We dined with the Claude and Rembrandt before us, breakfasted with the Rubens' landscape,'[1] said Haydon of his Coleorton visit, 'and did nothing, morning, noon or night, but think of painting, talk of painting, dream of painting, and wake to paint again.' Sir George was a painter of talent and tremendous industry – more than two thousand of his pictures still survive – but a modern critic would agree with Redgrave's

---

[1] Benjamin Robert Haydon (1786–1846), historical painter, was one of the first to recognize the importance of the Elgin marbles. He suffered much poverty and some neglect, and finally committed suicide in front of an early portrait of his wife, which he had hung on an easel before him.

slightly acid verdict that his landscapes 'did not surpass respectability in manner'; his scenes are often histrionic in conception and flat in colour. They were hung in the Royal Academy's exhibitions and politely praised by his contemporaries, often with genuine conviction; Constable himself speaks approvingly of 'a beautiful little landscape' which Sir George had painted for him: but of the two once possessed by the National Gallery one has decayed into total ruin without much remark, and the other is stored in the vaults of the Tate — a sad instance of ingratitude to its founder, but little loss, one must admit, to the public. His drawings, on the other hand, are sometimes highly skilled in execution, and fresh and spontaneous in their treatment, revealing a lively and observant mind, a keen eye, and an intimate love of natural objects. Cunningham speaks gently of the disparity between conception and execution.

He loved Claude, and imagined that he imitated him. His heart was, however, with Wilson; if he set up the former for his model, his eye wandered unconsciously to the latter. In his works, there is less of the fine fresh glow of nature than I could wish to see: there are glimpses of grandeur: indications rather than realities — the dawn, but never the full day. Yet nature had bestowed on him the soul and eye of a fine landscape painter; scenes shone on his fancy, which his hand had not the skill to embody: he saw paradise, with angels walking in glory among the trees; but the vision either passed away, or was dimly outlined on the canvas. Nature had done much for him; but fortune rendered the gift unavailing.

Wilkie[1] described him as 'a man whom nature had designed for a great painter but whom high fortune had marred'.

Sir George, however, modest and unassuming though he was, seemed happily unaware of how far he fell short of his own ambitions. Day after day he indulged his passion, en-

[1] Sir David Wilkie, R.A. (1785–1841), son of a Scottish manse. He became R.A. in 1811, succeeded Lawrence as painter-in-ordinary to the King in 1830, and was knighted in 1836.

thusiastic and content, the rare example of a truly happy man. He was indeed a man of genius too, but not in the manner he would have wished to suppose. His gift was less in the execution of art than its encouragement; in a discerning judgment, a generous capacity to praise as well as help, a highly cultivated taste, and above all an exceptional capacity for friendship which gave to the relationships between himself and men of humbler birth an ease and spontaneous warmth which few could achieve in the aristocratic England of the Regency. He could receive as well as give; and he was blessed with a wife whose sweetness of disposition and ready kindness were equal to his own. 'Both she and Sir George,' wrote Dorothy Wordsworth to her friend Catherine Clarkson, 'are human-hearted creatures, even as if they had been bred up and passed their lives among the best people of our own rank.' Paradoxically there is far less class consciousness and resentful snobbery in a society based upon clear-cut social distinctions than in one where everyone is assiduously anxious to pretend that they don't exist; and the Beaumonts had the grace and simplicity which recognized an equality of esteem despite all disparity of rank. Sir George argued that 'pride of intercourse' was as often the fault of the too humble as of the man of greater place. 'Each should be easy and let things take their course . . . As much pride is shown in keeping at a distance from apprehension of being rejected as in rejecting; both are to blame.' Sir George retained indeed some fine quality of his Elizabethan counterpart, which his ancestor Francis Beaumont would have recognized as 'magnanimity'. The resemblance suggested itself spontaneously to the minds of men as unalike as Coleridge and Cunningham. 'He had all the dignity which we assign to the Sidneys and Raleghs of Elizabeth's court, united to the polished elegance of that of George IV,' said the latter; while to Coleridge he showed 'what, and how much, is comprised in the phrase "a perfect gentleman" – but (let me add this necessary comment) as Edmund Spenser sang, and Sidney realized the idea'. He had the natural dignity which enabled him to meet freely and equally with all men while never becoming commonplace.

Small wonder that so many people delighted in the sunshine kindliness of the Beaumonts' hospitality, whether in London or the country. In the richness and variety of the talent that they drew to themselves they again remind one of the Sidneys. In their company George Dance would discuss his designs with Samuel Rogers, the banker-poet, and Angerstein, the banker-connoisseur. Royal Academicians dined with the Beaumonts' country neighbours and gossiped about those who seemed odd even in that age of great eccentrics – such as Sir Henry Harpur Crewe, who was so shy that he delivered his orders to his servants by letter, and nightly sat down alone at a table covered for several persons, though he allowed no servant to wait in the room. Sir Thomas Lawrence, the portrait painter, or Benjamin West, the President of the Royal Academy, would meet Wyndham, the Secretary for War. Humphry Davy, later the inventor of the miner's safety lamp, was welcome there, his thin dark face alight as he talked about his latest experiments to Coleridge or Wordsworth – for any suggestion of two cultures would greatly have perplexed Sir George's circle. Everyone in it was fascinated by Davy's discovery of nitrous oxide ('laughing gas') which he had managed to isolate, and which he called 'pleasure producing air'; and they submitted themselves with reckless readiness to prove its effects and record their sensations. Sir George himself was a fellow of the Royal Society. Davy had already discarded the eighteenth-century idea of 'phlogiston', the stuff of flame; but it was so firmly embedded in popular terminology that Coleridge once accused an enraged Southey of having phlogiston in his heart. Davy made scientists of his poet friends and learned from them a Wordsworthian vision of the world.

Today, for the first time in my life, I have had a distinct sympathy with nature. I was lying on the top of a rock to leeward; the wind was high, and everything was in motion. . . . Everything was alive, and I myself part of the series of visible impressions; I should have felt pain in tearing a leaf from one of the trees.

He wrote occasional poems himself, and described Coleridge in terms of romantic enthusiasm which remind one of the latter's own notebooks: 'Brilliant images of greatness float upon the mind, like images of the morning clouds on the waters.' He had his own scientific interest in art as well: while visiting Rome and Naples he experimented to find the nature and composition of the colours used by the ancient Greeks and Romans, and in 1815 presented his findings in a paper which he read to the Royal Society.

All were welcome at the Beaumonts' table, whether their lineage was as noble as Lord Lonsdale's or as humble as John Constable's. We have it on Dorothy Wordsworth's authority that Charles and Mary Lamb, too, 'knew and highly valued them'; and Crabbe was present on at least one occasion related by Sir Walter Scott, when he firmly extinguished the 'undulating thread of smoke' from an expiring candle which Sir George and Wordsworth were admiring; Scott would have thought their pleasure in it an affectation, were not Sir George an exquisite painter and 'the man in the world most void of affectation'.

Beaumont's good humour, his dry ironic wit, his droll manner of telling a good story, made him a popular host. Bannister, the actor, was one of those who dined with him before the theatre in a company that included Hoppner and Lord Mulgrave, when the occasion was so pleasant that a dining club was proposed so that it might be often repeated. Sir George never lost his lively enthusiasm for the theatre. He had known Garrick, and believed – as most of his contemporaries did – that no successor could equal him. He admired Kean, whose style of acting he preferred to the Kembles', but still tried to show him how Garrick had played Kitely in *Every Man in his Humour* and urged him to follow his example. There is – perhaps fortunately – no record of how the professional received this helpful advice from an amateur, but Sir George was disappointed when he saw Kean's performance. Mrs Siddons, he thought, owed most of her fame to her figure, countenance, and deportment; she was not a woman of superior understanding. But even he was a little overawed when face to face with her formidable personality. Haydon recounts how everyone hesitated to pronounce upon his 'Jerusalem' picture when it was exhibited until

in walked, with all the dignity of her majestic presence, Mrs Siddons, like a Ceres or a Juno. The whole room remained dead silent, and allowed her to think. After a few minutes Sir George Beaumont, who was extremely anxious, said in a very delicate manner: 'How do you like the Christ?' Everybody listened for her reply. After a moment, in a deep, loud, tragic tone, she said: 'It is completely successful.' I was then presented with all the ceremonies of a levée, and she invited me to her house in an awful tone.

What could the amiable Sir George do against a personality so powerful that it cowed even the most famous, as on the evening when Haydon was one of those invited to her house to hear her read *Macbeth*.

It is extraordinary the awe this wonderful woman inspires. After her first reading the men retired to tea. While we were all eating toast and tingling cups and saucers, she began again. It was like the effect of a mass bell at Madrid. All noise ceased; we slunk to our seats like boors, two or three of the most distinguished men of the day, with the very toast in their mouths, afraid to bite. It was curious to see Lawrence in this predicament, to hear him bite by degrees, and then stop for fear of making too much crackle, his eyes full of water from the constraint; and at the same time to hear Mrs Siddons' 'eye of newt and toe of frog!' and then to see Lawrence give a sly bite, and then look awed and pretend to be listening.

Actors, statesmen, poets, peers, artists, scientists, all formed a part of the Beaumonts' circle. What better ground could there be for the exchange of ideas and the fame of new talents?

One would achieve little by a careful, chronological account of Sir George's mature life. It is not the minutiae of events which are interesting, but the quality of this serene, uncluttered existence, the picture which emerges of himself and his wife as persons still so distinct and lively, yet so much a part of their age. The letters and journals of those who knew them reveal both in a room of slightly distorting mirrors, each of which alters the impressions given by the others; but the distortions are as fascinating as the likenesses, each of them revealing the writer as much as the subject.

There are six main sources, as well as a wealth of scattered references. The interminable diaries of Joseph Farington, R.A.,[1] are a mine of fact and gossip, sometimes malicious, frequently trivial, endlessly entertaining. This waspish egotist was nicknamed 'the Dictator of the Academy' because, as Northcote said, 'his great passion was the love of power – he loved to rule'. Farington was chiefly a topographical artist, whose paintings are now mostly forgotten; but he was an indefatigable eater at other men's tables, who recorded everything he could remember of every day. As a middle-aged and established artist he received nothing from the Beaumonts but hospitality, and an occasional discreet sneer suggests the jealousy of one who watches commissions going to younger, unknown men. He writes with the dry detachment of the completely self-centred.

Allan Cunningham, the enthusiast, is sometimes as unconsciously flattering as Farington is acid. Cunningham chronicles the lives of his contemporary artists with a breadth of generous sympathy which would willingly suppress any fault. He has the gift of admiration without envy; and if he is a little dazzled by wealth and consequence, he is also so guileless and so capable of disinterested love that he seems a sincerer witness than Farington.

[1] Joseph Farington, R.A. (1747–1821), landscape painter, a pupil of Richard Wilson.

Haydon is another egocentric, but of a nobler kind. His self-preoccupation derives from a genuine belief that he was one of the greatest of painters, so that he is prepared to sacrifice money, health, and family to the service of what he always calls 'the art'. He balances on the precarious edge of sanity, and his judgment of friends and patrons swings between extremes according to the chequered history of his own artistic fortunes. C. R. Leslie,[1] too, respects Beaumont for his services to contemporary artists, but his jealousy for his friend Constable's reputation makes his judgment disingenuous.

From these four we can gain a hundred fascinating glimpses of Sir George's life, but probably we see him most like himself if we balance the impressions of the two men who knew him best among all those who received his kindness – Coleridge and Wordsworth – Coleridge with his quick, generous, ardent, yet too facile enthusiasm, and Wordsworth the independent egocentric, more reserved than Coleridge, but with a capacity for strong and profound attachments.

The Sir George and Lady Beaumont who emerge from so much corroborating or conflicting evidence are in some ways wholly of the eighteenth century. For all his modest courtesy of manner, the baronet was sensitively aware of his family's distinction, its ancient history and noble blood, though characteristically he boasted of only one of his ancestors, and that for his gifts and not his birth. His greatest pride was that the Elizabethan dramatist, Francis Beaumont, had been one of his forebears and had lived at Grace Dieu among the rocks of Charnwood, close to Coleorton. He knew how to meet his inferiors as if they were his equals, could acknowledge their superior gifts, and would most certainly have admitted them to be as important as himself in any absolute scale of values. He was not a reformer or a new democrat, and he accepted his own social consequence as natural and inevitable advantages. In this he belonged to the untroubled, unquestioning social

---

[1] Charles Robert Leslie, R.A. (1794–1859), American painter domiciled in England, author of *Memoirs of the Life of John Constable*, 1848.

order of his youth; but with this implicit family pride went also the responsibility of a man of rank. When he rebuilt Coleorton he paid as much attention to the two villages and their cottages as to the hall itself. 'It was his pleasure to be acquainted with all who lived under his protection: and comfortable homes and happy tenants spoke of a wise as well as an indulgent master.' Whether as a country gentleman and his lady, or as members of a fashionable London circle, both Beaumonts belong to the world of Lord Chesterfield and Sir Joshua Reynolds. Yet in their private relationships, their enthusiasm, their sensibilities, they are wholly of the new Romantic movement. Lady Beaumont, especially, belongs to the new world of quick and eager response to whatever stirs the feelings, spontaneous joy or grief, emphatic delight. Revealingly Coleridge compares her to Dorothy Wordsworth – she 'has a soul in point of quick enthusiastic feeling, most like to Dorothy's'. Elsewhere he 'can describe her in few words – She is a miniature of Madame Guion

> *A deep Enthusiast, sensitive,*
> *Trembles and cannot keep the Tears in her eye –*
> *Such ones do love the marvellous too well*
> *Not to believe it. You may wind her up*
> *With any Music! –*

but *music* it must be, of some sort or other'. In some ways the Beaumonts even remind us of how near the world of the Regency was to that of Victorian England. Dr Bell's new monitorial system of education was already in existence. In 1808 the Dunmow trustees were in process of reorganizing the school, fixing the master's salary, and appropriating the parish house as a school building. Coleridge wrote to Dr Bell, full of enthusiasm, hopeful that he could interest the Beaumonts in the methods recently advocated in the latter's *The Madras School, or Elements of Tuition*; and a week later was happy to report their wish to consult the educationist about the school at Dunmow.

In this interest in good works, and in their quiet religious faith, they showed those qualities that were to be the strength of Victorian achievement. There is no evidence that they belonged to the Clapham Sect of Evangelical reformers, but they would have sympathized with its ideals. One of its chief leaders, Wilberforce, was well known to the Wordsworths, with whom he had stayed long before they knew the Beaumonts; and Wordsworth often writes to Sir George with an unselfconscious intimacy of religious feeling which assumes his correspondent's sympathy:

I look abroad upon Nature, I think of the best part of our Species, I lean upon my Friends, and I meditate upon the Scriptures, especially the Gospel of St John, and my creed rises up of itself with the ease of an exhalation, yet a fabric of adamant.

But he can also entertain his patron with amusing strictures upon the preacher at Coleorton, delivering to his village congregation 'a most knowing discourse about the Gnostics, and other hard names of those who were *h*adversaries of Christianity and *h*enemies of the Gospel'. In their later years the Beaumonts became increasingly interested in their parish church. In 1818 Sir George presented it with chalices, a flagon, and a paten; and he would certainly have contributed to the rebuilding of the spire and the repair of the tower in 1821, and the cost of the three new bells which in 1826 were added to the three already in the church.

They were too liberal and warm, too rooted in eighteenth-century common-sense, to be unnecessarily prudish, but their morality was firmly based. They sometimes deplored the laxity of public morals, and Sir George regretted the ease with which some women of fashion, no better than they should be, were admitted to public life. He attributed it partly to the ill example set by Charles Fox in bringing into society his ex-mistress, Mrs Arnstead, 'a woman who had been very common' before he married her. But among their acquaintances were glimpses of the modesty which was to drape even the legs of a Victorian sofa. That enthusiastic poet, the Rev William Bowles, was distressed by the close of Wordsworth's sonnet on the winter garden at Coleorton.

Be present as the music and the bloom
And all the mighty ravishment of spring.

Wordsworth defended the 'indelicate' word in the last line by the example of Milton himself, yet was nearly moved to suppress the whole sonnet to avoid such offence to his reverend critic. The Victorian Sunday also begins to cast a long shadow before, and Sir George would never enter his painting room on a Sunday nor trust himself with a portfolio. But if this quiet and sincere devotion was the secret source of much of their generosity, the Beaumonts were so endowed also with the social grace and gaiety of the Regency that only their intimates could be aware of these more sober traits.

There were no greater nor more practical friends to struggling artists. Sir George would commission a new work sooner than insult an artist's sense of independence by an unearned gift, and extended little acts of friendship that no one, however touchy, could resent. When Wilkie, ill and unable to work, refused his proffer of £100, he sent three dozen of his famous port instead, with a charming excuse that made rejection impossible.

It is not in the power of man to colour well, or indeed, to paint with effect, if his port wine is not good; I have therefore taken the liberty of sending you a few bottles of such as you cannot get at the retailers. A pleasant summer to you, and all the success you can wish.

In a hundred such instances of tact he proves the truth of Cunningham's praise that 'he was a gentleman in all that affected the feelings of men of genius'. To those whom they knew less well they extended the same ready help. They knew something of Julius Caesar Ibbetson, the ship's painter who became a landscape and figure artist, the father of a large family brought up in a life of misfortunes, debts, duns, and dissipation. Eight of the children died in quick succession, followed in 1794 by their exhausted mother. Three children still survived and, for one of them, a daughter, the Beaumonts made themselves responsible. When William Woollett's widow and daughters were found to be in need, Sir George remembered the man from whom he had learned in that long summer before his Oxford days, and was forward in organizing a subscription for them; and he was one of the small group of faithful friends who maintained J. R. Cozens during the insanity of his last sad years. Lady Beaumont delighted in small spontaneous kindnesses, quick to send gifts of money when Dorothy Wordsworth wrote of a 'statesman's' family suddenly orphaned or an old servant neglected.

They were ready too to use their influence among political friends, in a period when such influence was for many young men in the services their only hope of preferment – except for the few lucky enough to distinguish themselves exceptionally in active combat. Such preferment was too often for sale, but it was enough for the Beaumonts to be told of any young man of merit. Through their kindly and active interest, Southey's brother was promoted to the command of the brig *Lyra*, Southey himself obtained the post of King's Historiographer, and Wordsworth's brother-in-law, Henry Hutchinson, obtained his discharge as an exchanged prisoner-of-war after a series of adventures which should have been related in a Byronic epic. Even Farington solicited their help towards the advancement of his nephew in the navy. Ungracious as ever, he admitted almost reluctantly that 'Lady Beaumont was quite hearty in the business'. The nephew's command came more promptly than the uncle's gratitude. To the Southeys he was always kind, but his acquaintance with them lacked intimacy even though they also became guests at Coleorton. Southey wrote to him in a tone of polite deference, and signed himself 'Yours very respectfully' rather than with the natural affection of Wordsworth or Coleridge.

No one denies the Beaumonts' generosity, but when they appear as patrons of art it is indeed in a hall of mirrors. Those who benefited most had no doubt of their continuing kindness, and the better painters they were the more they could discuss their work with Sir George without resenting his comments as impertinence; but one or two of the older Academicians, jealous of his influence, indulged themselves in backbiting when they could. Farington watched for every sign that he could possibly interpret as a change of favour, and from time to time confided to his diary his conviction that an old protégé was being displaced by a new. He must often have been disappointed when both men continued in Sir George's friendship for many years to come. Northcote too, hearing that the baronet had 'taken up' with Wilkie, commented with his usual impish malignity: 'So then, he is to have a ride in the Flying Coach this year.' 'Wilkie is on the decline in favour,' Farington entered with cold satisfaction, in the spring of 1809. But Wilkie's own journal of the same period is full of friendly meetings and small courtesies to him, and in the same summer he was staying as a warmly welcomed guest at Coleorton.

Such critics made the most of Haydon's violent altercation with his patron, but they were too tough to understand Sir George's constitutional hatred of scenes, which was not merely a selfish withdrawal from disturbance. Both Beaumonts suffered from that kind of nervous sensibility which occurs so often among their contemporaries, perhaps the inevitable corollary of the aesthetic and moral sensibility which distinguished the best of their poetry and art. In its more neurotic form it was as characteristic of the period as melancholy was of the Elizabethans. Both were cultivated – and laughed at – as fashionable attitudes, but both had their correspondence in real life. In Sir George's case there may have been an additional physical cause. From time to time he spoke of 'one of his slow fevers' with the kind of familiar and proprietary respect that Mrs Bennet showed for her nerves. He had the high cheekbones, the brilliant eyes, and the bright colouring which so often go with tuberculosis, and one wonders what were the effects of those long immersions in the river at Eton. His emotional volatility suggests the same possibility, and Lady Beaumont's spirits seem to have waited very much upon his. Both were subject to times of intense depression. Sir George fussed a little about his health, wondered how much wine he should drink – he was indeed very abstemious – experimented with washing all over with cold water, though not with total immersion, took quantities of pills; oddly enough he seems never to have taken up the fashionable craze for sea-bathing, although in 1794 he visited Cheltenham, presumably to take the waters. In a childless and devoted marriage, Lady Beaumont tended to reflect his more despondent moods with a too keen sympathy of feeling.

But only his old friends were allowed to see the moments of low spirits. In company both of them were famous for their gaiety and charm, and they delighted in hospitality. He is 'playful, even boyish' at times, while Lady Beaumont's gift as a listener, her slight, engaging stammer when excited, her vivacity and sweetness of manner, made her a hostess loved and long remembered. So they moved among the circle of painters, writers, and gentlemen of fashion, who made their world, respected as patrons because they were also friends, having the power of money but none of its insolence, receiving pleasure where they gave kindness. None could have made better use of all the advantages that birth and wealth and influence could give them.

CHAPTER VI

The Feelings of Men of Genius

As a successful amateur, his own gifts sufficiently praised by connoisseurs to assure him of their existence, Sir George took a kindly interest in promising and humble aspirants to the arts as well as in established painters. In 1802 he and his friend, Lord Mulgrave, 'discovered' John Jackson, the son of a respectable tailor in Whitby, and apprenticed to the same trade. Haydon gives a colourful account of how Beaumont first met the young man at Mulgrave Castle and encouraged him to copy a Reynolds, taken from a picture by George Colman, using – in the absence of proper materials – house painter's brushes, vandyke brown from the woods, Indian red obtained from the alum works by burning, yellow ochre from the local mud, and a blue-black from soot. The ebullient and kindly Jackson loved to please, and he no doubt knew how Haydon relished such a story. It would be pleasant to believe it; but a letter from Sir George to Lord Mulgrave suggests that Cunningham's more sober narrative is also more accurate, and that Mulgrave saw the young man's sketches and passed them on to Beaumont for his more informed opinion. He writes with the disinterested helpfulness of the expert to a young beginner.

The young man seems to have great feeling for the simplicity of nature, and I have no doubt but he will succeed. At present, as might be expected, they are deficient in drawing, and I would recommend it to him to abate his velocity and to aim at correctness.

He would advise attendance at the Royal Academy rather than apprenticeship to an established artist. Soon after this, Sir George and Lord Mulgrave between them purchased the remaining two years of Jackson's unexpired apprenticeship, and brought the young painter to London, where Lord Mulgrave allowed him a yearly pension of £50, and the Beaumonts gave him frequent hospitality. But Jackson seems to have 'abated his velocity' much too completely, and later letters between his two patrons are full of anxious complaints about his lack of application and his apathy. At one point Lord Mulgrave was even driven to cut off his allowance for a while in order to compel him to depend upon his own exertions. Jackson responded cheerfully and without resentment, and the pension was renewed (though Haydon characteristically forgets to mention it); but his love of gossip and play was incorrigible. He would rather stand for hours 'with one hand in his trousers' pocket', telling his fund of Yorkshire stories 'full of nature and tact, racy and beautiful', or wandering in Vauxhall or Covent Garden in search of 'expression and effect' rather than in working at his easel. His patrons regarded his indolence with mingled indignation and amusement, but continued their support with a kind of resigned disapproval. Throughout their long acquaintance Sir George maintained always the manner of a patron, kindly, accessible, affable, but always feeling qualified to advise. He considered it even his duty to Lord Mulgrave to criticize the young man's work and impel him to fresh efforts.

But when in 1806, Jackson generously introduced David Wilkie to Sir George, a very different kind of relationship was initiated. Beaumont's youthful taste had been formed by Reynolds, and his heart was with the great artists of the past. He encouraged contemporary painters but distrusted any verdict on their value, as likely to be disproved by time; nor was he above the preferences and prejudices of his own day. Yet there was justice in Cunningham's claim that 'he was the best judge of pictures I ever remember'. Jackson was rarely more than a mediocre painter; but Wilkie had genius, however much he may now be out of fashion, and Beaumont realized it at a first meeting. The tall thin Scotsman, still only twenty,

10. *Sketch Portrait of Joseph Farington, R.A.*,
by George Dance

11. *Sir Humphry Davy*, by James Sharples

12. *Sir David Wilkie*, by Sir William Beechey

13. *Benjamin Robert Haydon*, by Georgiana Zornlin

had left his father's manse some months before and was living
chiefly on hope. He had just completed his *Village Politicians*,
commissioned by Lord Mansfield; and Jackson, always richer
in heart than genius, generously brought the picture to the
notice of his own two patrons. Sir George recognized in it
at once a new idiom and a new genius. Full of enthusiasm
he commissioned a picture himself (*The Blind Fiddler*), and
inspired Lord Mulgrave to do the same. But with his own
sensitive gift for friendship he also recognized something else
in this young, pale Scot, with the awkward manner, and his
wrists protruding from his ancient jacket – saw in him the
genuine devotion to art and the delicacy of honourable feeling
in which he so much resembled his new patron. He would
have delighted had he known of it in the portentous secret
revealed to Haydon at a tea-party which celebrated Wilkie's
first success.

Something of vast importance was brewing, we could not
imagine what. . . . He took me into another room, and there –
spread out in glittering triumph – were two new bonnets, two new
shawls, ribbons and satins, and Heaven knows what, to astonish the
natives of Cults, and to enable Wilkie's venerable father, like the
Vicar of Wakefield, to preach a sermon on the vanity of women,
whilst his wife and daughter were shining in the splendour of
fashion from the dressmakers at the west end of London . . . ! Then
came the packing; then the dangers by sea, and the dangers by
land; then the landlady and her daughter, and all her friends, were
in consultation deep, and profound were the discussions how to
secure 'those sweet bonnets from being crushed' and 'those charming ribbons from sea-water'. . . . All the time Wilkie stood by,
eager and interested beyond belief, till his conscience began to prick
him, and he said to me: 'I have jest been very idle,' and so for a
couple of days he set to, heart and soul, at *The Blind Fiddler* for
Sir George.

Sir George knew nothing of this little scene; but he was one
of the very few who discerned the capacity for warmth and
gentleness beneath Wilkie's rather unpromising exterior.

Towards Jackson he was no more than kind, but Wilkie struck a personal response from him, which he expressed in a symbolic and romantic gesture. Amongst his most cherished possessions had been Hogarth's own mahl stick; but on seeing *The Village Politicians* he impulsively presented it to this raw young man as a painter worthy to possess it.

The gift marked the beginning of a very genuine friendship. Where Sir George's liking was once engaged, he proved the most faithful of benefactors, and the long years of association with Wilkie show both the Beaumonts at their best in generosity and delicacy of spirit. Wilkie certainly needed a delicate approach, especially in the earlier years, when he was poor, often sick, proud, and sensitive as a snail's horns. Soon after he had commissioned *The Blind Fiddler* and *The Gamekeeper*, Sir George made a second attempt to pay the artist in advance, but in terms that could suggest no hint of charity.

When I was in town I hinted to you that I was perfectly ready to advance any money, even to the full price of the two pictures, if it would be any accommodation to you: you declined it, I suspect through delicacy; I therefore repeat my offer, and sincerely assure you, that, as my wish is to serve you, I shall consider your receiving the money as no obligation whatever. I only fear you may be put to inconvenience, or lay yourself under an obligation to someone who may give you trouble hereafter, or take some advantage of your situation. You will pardon me if I am mistaken, as I know no more of your concerns than has accidentally dropt from Mr Jackson.

In November of the same year he is still trying to help, but with sympathy so alert that he can be as generous in withdrawal as in giving. He writes to Lord Mulgrave:

You will certainly think the devil is in me for writing, yet I cannot refrain from telling you what passed on my visit to Wilkie which I made just after I had sent your letter. – He positively refused to accept a farthing more than I had already given him, & on my pressing him with all my might, I perceived he had actually

[82]

tears in his eyes, & I am confident nothing short of my telling him I should be hurt and offended would have prevailed. This in my zeal I was about to do, when I recollected I was preventing him from doing a noble and disinterested thing, not to give him pleasure but pain, for my own gratification, & I forbore.

Wilkie's art was in a field which Sir George himself never attempted, *genre* painting of ordinary simple people. His peasants are neither Hogarthian caricatures not the idealized rustics of a Poussin or Claude, but as real as the poor of his father's parish who had been his first models. 'Heroic' painters, jealous of his early success, sneered at his 'pan and spoon' style; but his figures have freshness, vitality, and humour, and his simple, episodic subjects appealed to the romantic vein of sentiment. He reveals them with neither the pity nor the reverence which Wordsworth showed for humble people, yet with a canny understanding.

As long as these were his subject, Beaumont offered little comment other than admiration. But when his young protégé attempted the heroic theme of 'Alfred in the Neatherd's Hut' while his reputation was still in the making, he felt himself entitled to give advice as well as encouragement; his own years of study and devotion qualified him to speak. It could hardly be considered an impertinence in one of his authority in the world of taste, and like many an amateur enthusiast he knew what he was talking about even if his own execution was weak.

The critic was strong (says Cunningham) where the artist was weak. He was a scholar as well as a man of taste; descended too from a line of kings and emperors; conversant with the history and character of the times, of which the artist desired to give a lively image; and, more than all, had much of that loftiness of soul which the man must share in who paints kings and heroes.

Sir George complained of the insipidity of Wilkie's Alfred compared with the neatherd's family, and wished for the sake of decorum that the peasants should be softened and idealized to suit the heroic theme.

You will recollect that much glory surrounds the character of Alfred – that any situation, however mean in itself, receives dignity from him: the story, if I may so express myself, should be told in blank verse. Whatever may have been the fact, a certain classical veil should be thrown over each trivial circumstance; and it is upon this ground I rather object at present to the expression of the girl who is taking up the cakes, as a little too ludicrous. The same natural manner of taking them up, nay, the same expression of countenance, may be preserved, only it should be softened, and the face more refined and delicate.

Wilkie's reply shows how little he resented the criticism, and how deeply he was imbued with the ideas of Burke and Reynolds. He agrees that his patron's remarks are 'extremely just'.

As the principal object in an historical composition is to lead the mind back to the time in which the transaction happened, and the mind being always ready to associate elevated ideas with antiquity, the illusion must be instantly destroyed, and the purpose of the picture entirely defeated, if the vulgar familiarity of the circumstances instantly puts us in mind of what passes every day before our eyes.

There is nothing here to alarm the most conservative of patrons. Wilkie accepted without question Beaumont's own early canons of taste. He was very conscious of an imaginative relationship between poetry and painting, and allowed Sir George to guide his reading.

You should enrich your mind (writes the latter) by the study of our best authors, especially the poets. You can never read Shakespeare, Milton, and Spenser too much. Some of our best novelists, as Richardson, Fielding and Smollett, are also worthy of your attention. Don Quixote I particularly recommend: let him lie upon your table, and read a chapter when you are fatigued with your work; it will refresh and improve your mind.

Yet while stressing the essentially poetic nature of painting, Beaumont warned his young friend against too close a dependence upon a specifically literary inspiration. The Duke of Wellington had commissioned a picture of a group of old soldiers recounting their stories to each other as they sit outside the door of an inn, and Sir George was pleased to hear of it.

I think I remember an excellent description in Goldsmith's *Deserted Village* of an old soldier shouldering his crutch and describing his actions to his family and friends on his return from the wars. I mention this because I think anything analogous to what we are about, well treated in poetry, animates and illuminates the mind . . . [but] the painter had better be the author of his own subject; for if the poet from whom he takes his ideas be a moderate one, he had certainly better trust to himself; and if he be excellent, the mind of the spectator is prejudiced. . . . It is indeed almost impossible to contend successfully with a strong previous impression.

One catches an echo of John Boydell's catalogue of the pictures in the Shakespeare Gallery in Pall Mall in 1789, quoted in the *Gentlemen's Magazine*, that dignified repository of contemporary taste. 'It must not then be expected that the art of the painter can ever equal the sublimity of our poet.' (Not that this prevented the painter from trying! The Royal Shakespeare Theatre Picture Gallery has a rich collection of eighteenth and nineteenth century paintings on Shakespearean themes, which survive from the vast number which appeared in the exhibitions every year. It was the great age of 'Bardolatry'.)

The letters between Beaumont and Wilkie are not only about painting. Sir George's care was for the friend as much as the artist, and he was deeply concerned during the young man's long illness. He offered financial help with the utmost delicacy, and arranged that Wilkie should stay in the fresh air of Hampstead under the care of his fellow-Scot, Dr Matthew Baillie. Baillie's sister Joanna, the poetess and dramatist,[1] was a 'good friend' of the Beaumonts, and she and her sister would look after the invalid. Later Wilkie came to Dunmow to complete his convalescence under the cherishing kindness of Lady Beaumont – paying only the small price of listening to her readings of Wordsworth's poetry, which he was much too conservative to admire, so that he 'could not be brought at all to coincide with the fundamental principles of his system'. Shy though he was, 'silent as the grave and as proud as Lucifer', as a fellow artist once described him, he responded with all the affection of his heart; he told Cunningham that 'when he met Sir George Beaumont or had a letter from him, he always studied with alacrity and cheerfulness for the rest of the day'.

Wilkie himself was a kind and generous friend. His letters never missed an opportunity to put in a word of praise for Jackson and Haydon, especially if he feared the slightest strain between his friends and their patron. He reported that the dilatory Jackson was 'giving very regular attendance at the Royal Academy', and that Haydon improved much in execution. His common-sense and moderation served the latter well during the vexed affair of his 'Macbeth' picture, in which nearly everyone in the Beaumont circle became at one time or another involved.

Haydon had come up to London some five years before this incident as a lad of eighteen. He was to win considerable admiration as a painter, despite his quarrels with nearly every man of influence in London; and his small repute today is largely because we have lost the taste for the kind of grandiose historical subject which he thought alone worthy of himself.

---

[1] Joanna Baillie (1762–1851), author of *Fugitive Verses*, 1790, and *Plays on the Passions*, 1798. Kemble produced her *De Montfort* at Drury Lane in 1800, with himself and Mrs Siddons in the chief parts, but the play ran only for eleven nights.

He had the highly coloured imagination of a romantic novelist, and with it he created the grotesque tragi-comedy of his own disastrous life. He saw himself as a rebel genius, a man of the people 'proud to sustain a quarrel with a man of rank', a devoted sacrifice to the integrity of art. He lived in a dream – sometimes a nightmare – of his own creation; yet because he honestly believed it to be reality, he does acquire a sort of tragic impressiveness: and as one turns the pages of his journal one watches with horrified pity his noisy, posturing rush down the dark tunnel of his self-delusions to the inevitable moment when with knife and pistol he inflicted his own death. He was a wholly impossible person, Malvolio trying to play Lear. He was arrogant and touchy towards his friends, and to his would-be patrons showing independence of spirit by the incivility of his address and suspicion of every kindness. Such was the man whom Wilkie, generous and patient, had introduced to Sir George Beaumont.

Both the patron and his new protégé were at first delighted. Sir George recognized the distinction of Haydon's painting, shared his enthusiasm for the great painters of the past as the only true masters, approved his preference for heroic themes, and felt his usual disinterested pleasure in encouraging a young man of great promise. Haydon was invited to Grosvenor Square, where Lady Beaumont charmed him on his first visit by listening to all his ambitions and drawing him to the attention of the company. A friend of the Beaumonts became always a friend of the Mulgraves, so to Harley Street also he went and, to prove his independence, on his first visit flatly contradicted Lord Mulgrave at his own table. But the awkward moment was courteously glossed over. Allowances had to be made for a young man whose sense of social inequality was only surpassed by his sense of his own genius. (In the privacy of his own journal Haydon was far more elated than Wilkie by his distinguished new acquaintances and the coaches that called at his door.) In the late summer of 1809 his long cherished hope came true, and he was invited to

Coleorton with Wilkie. For a rapturous fortnight the two artists and their host spent all the day in painting, 'unwillingly separated for the night, and arose with the lark to go at it again'. But even here Haydon was driven by his need to outshine the others. While they were making studies of the rocks at Charnwood, he secretly painted the head of one of Sir George's horses, 'full of life and fire', and 'bringing it in when the party assembled for dinner, had the satisfaction of demolishing their little bits of study, for the size of life, effectually done, is sure to carry off the prize'.

A happy visit to give rise to an absurd tragi-comic disaster, but so it did. During its course, Sir George commissioned a painting from *Macbeth*, and Haydon even began straightway on a study for Lady Macbeth from his hostess's maid, posing her on the stairs with the light behind her to cast her shadow.

He at once conceived his subject on the grandest possible scale though, if he had had an ear for tone, he might have recollected Sir George's slightly ambiguous comment on his first picture of 'Joseph and Mary' — 'very poetical, and quite large enough for anything.' But, alas, he listened to no voice but his own, and in fact made a point of ignoring advice as irrelevant or impertinent. 'Sir George told me,' he recounts on one occasion, 'Sir Joshua used white of egg, and advised me to do the same, with half a dozen other things, to all of which I paid no attention.' So once again Haydon chose not to notice any suggestion, but departed to London and began work. Sir George, arriving in town several weeks later, was startled to find an enormous canvas with nearly life-sized figures — so large, indeed, that the near approach to human height made them seem people real but slightly dwarfed — an uncomfortable illusion, which Wilkie also found disturbing. A request to reduce the size of the picture immediately filled the young artist with 'the glory of resistance to injustice', a heady and dangerous wine. There was a near-quarrel, Sir George left town to winter as usual at Dunmow, and letters passed to and fro, Haydon still asserting his own judgment and 'breathing like a young lion that had just burst the net which fettered him'; until at last the exhausted and irritated patron left this leonine fury to spend itself without reply. Meanwhile Haydon painted doggedly on, spending more and more money on the picture. Wilkie, called upon for advice and sympathy, begged his friend to consider smaller canvases if he ever hoped to sell them, and told him 'if he could overcome his own feelings and follow Sir George's advice, he was only sacrificing his own inclinations to public opinion.' But by this time Haydon was beyond reason; opposition at any time tended to rouse him to an almost paranoic self-assertiveness. He began to carry his complaints round the whole circle of his acquaintance, to Farington, who liked any suggestion that Sir George might be fickle, to Constable, to Northcote, who had always maliciously encouraged him to distrust his patron; and at last he even showed Beaumont's letters to other people, and wrote to Lord Mulgrave in a manner almost deranged, calling him his real patron, and demanding sympathy. Lord Mulgrave showed the letter to Beaumont, both of them feeling uneasy about the effects of so much excitement upon Haydon's unbalanced temperament. He was known to be neglecting all other occupation. In a last effort at understanding, the Beaumonts invited the desperate young man to dinner and tried to suggest to him the impropriety of his behaviour. But he only committed to his journal a fantastically self-inflated account of the evening, admitting that 'Lady Beaumont was enchanting', but absurdly pleased with himself for repulsing her efforts at reconciliation.

The dispute dragged miserably on, chiefly sustained by the artist's own fury. In Haydon's account Sir George appears a vain, capricious and quite heartless tyrant; in Farington's an uncertain and whimsical patron; and in Wilkie's a man of sorely tried common-sense. Haydon leaves the reader to suppose that the picture was left upon his hands, with a vast debt for the materials he had used. But the end of the affair is given in a letter from Sir George to Wilkie.

Your account of Haydon's progress gives me sincere pleasure: everything may be expected from him if he exerts himself uniformly; and such is his enthusiasm, I think there cannot be any doubt of that. You assuredly know that I have The Macbeth; for, although the size is a serious inconvenience to me, yet the picture remaining upon his hands gave me uneasiness; and upon his expressing his wish that I would take it instead of the one he was about to begin for me, I complied; for my first wish was to serve him. Indeed, excepting the size of the figure of Macbeth, in which he has however shown great power, although I think he has failed, the picture is very fine, the colouring is excellent, and many parts perhaps equal to anything he will ever do.

It is a fascinating picture of relationships – Northcote's chuckling malice, Farington's preference for a spice of scandal in his gossip, poor Haydon's incredible heroics, Wilkie's cool northern common-sense; and Sir George in the midst of it, hating scenes, torn between his sense of justice and exasperated astonishment. For a while he kept Haydon at a wise distance, perhaps with some sense of dignified displeasure. But his innate kindness always asserted itself, aided perhaps by the dry ironical humour with which he regarded 'the little jealousies and party bickerings' of artists and critics alike, which 'he held injurious to the dignity of art, and to the title of a gentleman'. Before long Haydon was again invited to his table, and the relationship was resumed, though with more caution on Sir George's part, and with undiminished kindness and practical aid.

Unfortunately Haydon was more apt to record supposed affronts than any subsequent reconciliation. Younger friends of his, such as Keats, knew Sir George only through his report, and spoke of him therefore with angry aversion. Poor Haydon had only one hero – himself. He could not speak, as Coleridge so often did, of 'his dear and honoured friend' – giving each word its absolute value – for he lacked that free and modest spirit which made Coleridge a great man even in his decline. But at the time when Keats made his stricture, Beaumont was doing all he could to persuade the British Gallery to buy Haydon's *Jerusalem* and, failing in that, was active in a scheme to buy it by subscription; and he had also obtained him a pupil whose fees might help to support him. But however little Haydon might say to his friends, his own affection had revived. His later journals speak often, long years after Beaumont's death, of how he 'bitterly lamented' his old patron – 'one of the old school formed by Sir Joshua – a link between the artist and the nobleman, elevating the one by an intimacy which did not depress the other'. He links his name with that of Lord Egremont of Petworth; 'at his table, as at Sir George Beaumont's . . . painter and sculptor, poet and minister and soldier, all were his equals'.

In Haydon's last thought of him, old affection won. In the tragic will written on the night of his suicide the artist makes his final salute to the patron.

The Duke of Sutherland, Lord Egremont, Lord Mulgrave, Sir George Beaumont, Sir Robert Peel, the late Thomas Kearsey, etc. etc., employed and helped me, and William Hamilton. God reward them!

CHAPTER VII

Painters of the English Scene

When in 1794 Mrs Constable took her son to the dowager Lady Beaumont's house in Dedham, she hoped merely to obtain the interest of a well-known patron. She had no idea that she was sounding a trumpet outside the walls of Jericho. Reynolds had died only two years before, portrait painting was that which led to profitable commissions, and 'historical' painters were those most revered by fashion and the establishment. These were the premises of art on which Sir George had been bred. But if, as Wordsworth later said, his own pencil was 'not untrue to common recognitions', he was to owe it at least in part to the shy young man now presented to him by a hopeful parent.

The seeds of change were growing quietly long before this meeting. Writers and dilettantes were showing an interest in 'Gothic' styles and medieval romances, with a nice taste in ancient ruins. Heroic painting itself evinced a kind of febrile enthusiasm far removed from the classical restraint of a mind, as Sir Joshua once described it, 'thrown back two thousands years, and, as it were, naturalized in antiquity, like that of Nicolo Poussin'. Haydon was to have more in common with Delacroix than with the Old Masters whom he thought himself to emulate. But Sir George was still in the world of the eighteenth century. His attitude to Gothic was very much that of Walpole himself, one of amused enjoyment. Writing to his friend Lord Mulgrave, he teases his little godson on being an infant Monk Lewis.[1]

I have no doubt but my little godson can write better than

[1] Matthew Gregory Lewis (1775–1818), whose *The Monk* was one of the most notorious of 'Gothic' romances.

spectre Lewis already, and I should not be surprised if he should reverse the common order of things and frighten his nurse out of her senses with tales of wonder, before the month is up. I know I should not like to be in his way when he comes to be inspired.

The ruins that he chiefly approves are classical, not medieval – Poussin's or Claude's. Owls and ivy have as yet made no impression on him. The first generation of romantic artists and writers was only slightly drawn by the lure of the medieval which so fascinated Keats and the early Victorians. If they used a medieval setting, as Wordsworth did in *The White Doe of Rylstone* or Coleridge in *Christabel*, it was because its remoteness increased the sense of isolated concentration upon a moral theme of permanent importance. A more far-reaching and subtle influence than this was the change in their response to landscape and their awareness of human nature.

Gothic was a conscious affectation; but an Englishman's response to his natural environment is so much a part of himself and so taken for granted that he is hardly aware of any change until it is made fully explicit in art. There has never been a time when he took no pleasure in the natural scene. In the eighteenth century it was the hardly acknowledged pleasure which a man may take in his wife's company at breakfast after forty years of marriage – a companionable happiness of which he becomes aware only if it is removed. It was a profound relationship, which included the aesthetic, but went far beyond it. The local landscape made demands upon the inhabitants; its beauty was related to labour and harvest, and even the improver of the landscaped park had an eye upon the future value of timber. Even the climate had a wifely quality, temperate even when changeable, and lacking romance or drama. When an early eighteenth-century poet wanted to talk about the English scene – and he often did – he needed to do it only in the most general terms, to which his reader would respond with general though approving sentiments. (Even today, eighteenth-century nature poetry arouses less response in the heart of a townsman than in the heart of a country dweller, for whom a familiar symbol is enough to evoke a complex of happy associations.)

The inescapable quiet beauty of field and hedgerow, stream and scented garden, had indeed its own delicious charms, but it was not sublime – not unless one happened to live somewhere north of Manchester, and even there one found only a modified sublimity. And in the high eighteenth century only the sublime was fit material for art. For this one had to look abroad, to Italy or the Alps, to mountains and plunging waterfalls, beetling crags and bristling woods, where the word 'horrid' can be used in its full Miltonic dreadfulness – 'grots and caverns shagged with horrid shades'. Gray made do as well as he could with the Welsh mountains; but the Gothic romance, to be frightful enough, demands nothing less than the south of France at least, and Catherine Moreland does her best to imagine Alpine terrors in the gentle hills round Bath. This is the proper world of landscape art, in so far as the eighteenth century recognized it as art at all. It is as literary and poetic as heroic painting, and the interest is less in the scene itself than in the sublime emotions it can conjure up in the spectator. Italian lakes and mountains, dramatically lighted, waiting like a stage set for some vast Aeschylean tragedy, ruined aqueducts and temples in the mellow timeless light of another world, these were the subjects that the youthful Sir George was taught to regard as proper for his brush, and which he faithfully tried to present for the greater part of his life.

Yet looking at Beaumont's pencil sketches, one feels in them a more spontaneous response to things of beauty than in all his carefully contrived oils, common 'recognitions' of a world where sublimity is not the only criterion, a world that poets are already beginning to explore. The year of Richard Wilson's death, 1782, saw the publication of a small volume of poems by a hitherto unknown writer, William Cowper.

Gentle, sensitive, affectionate, clinging desperately to the normal over a pit of nightmare terrors, Cowper had no need of sublime objects to arouse a sense of awe. Convinced of his own eternal damnation, he took a temporary and precarious refuge in the quiet beauty of the Buckinghamshire countryside, restricting even this to his own garden and the narrow radius round it that could be reached in a morning's walk. In the best-loved of all his poems, *The Task*, written only a year after Wilson's death, he celebrated this quiet world with an exquisite precision of detail which makes the commonplace glitter like a spider's web after rain.

> *The redbreast warbles still, but is content*
> *With slender notes, and more than half suppress'd:*
> *Pleas'd with his solitude, and flitting light*
> *From spray to spray, where'er he rests he shakes*
> *From many a twig the pendent drops of ice,*
> *That tinkle in the wither'd leaves below.*
> *Stillness, accompanied with sounds so soft,*
> *Charms more than silence.*

This is the withdrawn yet intimate England celebrated by so many topographical artists, whose skill was employed to record the splendours of a rebuilt mansion, the new improvements to some great estate – regarded as skilled draughtsmen rather than artists, recorders rather than creators. Their numbers testify to the continued enthusiasm of the English gentry, small and great, for 'earth and mortar'. But just because these unpretentious watercolours were intended as a faithful record they led insensibly to a reversal of values. The steady contemplation of an English scene for its own sake evokes the profound affection and sympathy for it which seems inherent in our character. Those who began by taking a likeness, forerunners of the Victorian photographer, ended by painting English trees, English weather, English skies, painting not only the scene but the artist's love for it.

This was the love that Beaumont recognized in the studies

of Thomas Hearne – statements in prose perhaps, but prose
so lucidly and exquisitely wrought that it brings with it the
freshness of the morning air. This was exciting enough, but
in the younger Cozens he discovered a wholly new quality
in landscape. Here there is no careful grouping of trees,
buildings, and skies, to arouse sublime feelings by their
associations, as in some of Paul Sandby's compositions: in
Cozens the poetic feeling is already there, inherent in the
scene itself. His pictures, full of space and light and movement, stirred Sir George so deeply that at times his own work
unconsciously reflects them. Except for the darker and browner
colouring, there is an unmistakable echo in *Peele Castle in a
Storm* of Cozens' *Coast Scene between Vietri and Salerno*; a
dark curtain of clouds swirls with the same movement round
a central area of light, the sea dashes towards the rocks and
broken buildings to the left, and even the tormented ship
seems a memory of the little boat tossing helplessly near the
Italian coast. And meanwhile a greater than Hearne or Cozens
had learned to find his subject 'in every hedge and hollow
tree'; Gainsborough was at last revealing the *Englishness*
of English landscape.

With all his admiration for the great masters and his devotion to eighteenth-century ideals of the heroic and sublime,
Sir George was still aware of this new quality in English
art. Among the pictures he added to his own collection were
more than thirty watercolour drawings by Girtin, the first
which Constable ever saw. Here were pictures to reveal even
more clearly to the young painter the profoundly moving
quality of the commonplace. Looking at them, one can feel
the drugged warmth of summer in the very depth and weight
of his trees, and even know how the soft dried mud of the
lane will crumble with a faint dull sound beneath one's feet.
From him Constable could learn how to paint not only a
scene, but the intense affection which the scene arouses.

This recognition of poetic quality inherent even in simple
and familiar things, beginning so quietly in the work of

14. *Coast Scene between Vietri and Salerno*, by J. R. Cozens

15. *Peele Castle in a Storm*, by Sir George Beaumont

16. *William Wordsworth*, by Benjamin Robert Haydon

17. *Samuel Taylor Coleridge*, by James Northcote. Painted for Sir George Beaumont in 1804, and said to be 'very like'

Cowper and the topographical painters of Beaumont's youth, gained in momentum in his later life, and it was his own appreciation of it, despite all his early training and settled tastes, that showed the touch of genius as a patron.

At the end of the eighteenth century two forces were at work which combined to show the beauty of the common-place. One was the new political consciousness which was stirring in the whole of Europe, manifesting itself in revo-lution in France, and in the Reform Movement in England; the other the development of true romantic sensibility out of the mere indulgence of sentiment in the mid century. Poli-tical thought and aesthetic thought met on the common ground of moral consciousness. The evolution which the two were to work in English culture is clearly seen in the relation-ship of the Beaumonts with Constable on one hand, and with Coleridge and the Wordsworths on the other.

They were living – as most people do – in a society only half aware of its self-contradictions, which showed itself among thoughtful people in an uneasy awareness of the extremes of wealth and poverty, of the anomalies of the electoral system, of the need to feel some responsibility for the ignorant and oppressed, and to question the divine right and privilege of aristocracy and inherited power. But such stirrings of the social conscience were balanced by attachment to tradition and the way in which theoretical evils were modified in fact by personal relationships. The man of rank whose wealth supported a great estate and bought him a seat in Parliament was rarely a local tyrant, a grinder of the faces of the poor, a corrupt exploiter of his political opportunities. He was a man – like Sir George himself – who might be one of two members representing a single elector, but who voted honestly for measures which he believed to be good, and used his pri-vileges to obtain advancement for young men whose worth he thoroughly approved; who rebuilt his own house, but acted also as a responsible landlord with a care for his tenants' good; who used his wealth to satisfy his own tastes, but also

G

to encourage men of genius; who, above all, had personal and often friendly contact with his dependants.

It is this which lies at the root of the oddly ambivalent attitude of so many political writers of the reform period, such as the novelist Robert Bage.[1] The hero of Bage's *James Wallace*, for instance, is an impoverished young man who enters domestic service and wins the heroine's love while he is still her footman. But although she rejects wealthy suitors for his sake, and the two lovers sometimes talk of marriage despite all conventional barriers, they never really consider it; and the wedding is delayed until at last Wallace is discovered to be the heir to a wealthy baronetcy. His *Hermsprong, or Man as he is not*, which won quite a reputation in its own day and was much praised by Sir Walter Scott, has the same anomaly at heart. Hermsprong is the 'natural man' of the romantic imagination, the transatlantic democrat whose independent and noble spirit is contrasted with the arrogant heartlessness of Lord Grondale, the heroine's father. But it is not until Hermsprong reveals that he is really the son of Lord Grondale's elder brother and the rightful inheritor of his estates that he is able to marry his cousin. Bage is an adept at satisfying democratic principle without injury to aristocratic prejudice.

This was the world, poised on the edge of change, in which Beaumont and Constable first met. It seems to have been an amiable encounter, and Constable's delighted glimpse of Sir George's beloved Claude, the *Hagar* which he always carried with him, was his first acquaintance with a real painting by a great master; and he obtained leave to copy from the collection of Girtin drawings. Constable already felt that 'there was room enough for a natural painter', and Sir George once told Hoppner that 'he would give anything to see an accomplished Landscape Painter arise'. Why then was the public countenance that he gave to Constable so much more belated than that which he gave to Wilkie or Haydon?

[1] Robert Bage (1728–1801), Midland paper-maker who in his middle age became a novelist with democratic notions.

Two things stood in the way. Constable feared and resented a too exclusive devotion to the works of the Old Masters, which Sir George so often advocated. No man loved them more, but he hated the 'multitude of abortions' which were spawned by servile imitators. He saw in the collectors' passion for the darkening canvases of old paintings a threat to 'God Almighty's daylight, which is enjoyed by all mankind, excepting only the lovers of old dirty canvas, perished pictures at a thousand guineas each, cart grease, tar, and snuff of candle'. And his interpretation of landscape art was wholly different from his patron's.

Sir George's idea of landscape we know already. 'The beautiful style of art which he professed,' Wilkie wrote to Lady Beaumont after his patron's death, 'was abstract and general – a poetical recollection rather than a minute detail of nature; full of sentiment and feeling, and eminently successful in what was his chief delight – a rich and deep tone of colouring.' His pictures, with their carefully dramatic composition, the dark tones bordering a central area of light, their nostalgic reminiscences of Claude, are still of ideal landscapes, the very essence of which is summed up in Wordsworth's words on his *Peele Castle* – 'the consecration and the poet's dream'. But Constable saw nature with a much more direct and personal vision, and with the same kind of love that Cowper gave it. With him his sympathy was close.

I have all Cowper's works on my table. . . . He is an author I prefer to almost any other, and when with him I always feel the better for it. . . . He is the poet of religion and nature.

Later there was a rival in his affections when Fisher presented him with Gilbert White's *Selborne*. 'It shows what a real love of nature will do. . . . This book is an addition to my estate.' It is not fanciful to see in Constable's art the influence of his two favourite authors – he paints with the exquisite observation of White charged with the poetic intensity of Cowper. But his landscapes are not, like Poussin's or Claude's, nature enhanced, sublimed, translated by the artist's own poetic feeling. The poetry is inherent in the scene itself. 'Painting is with me but another word for feeling.' He was impatient of anything that might suggest the additions of fancy. Leslie tells the story of his dry retort to Blake who 'looking through one of Constable's sketch books, said of a beautiful drawing of an avenue of fir trees on Hampstead Heath, "Why, this is not drawing, but *inspiration*"; and he replied, "I never knew it before; I meant it for drawing".'

One wonders whether Sir George ever fully understood the subjects of Constable's art; for what the younger man painted was not natural objects so much as the daily phenomena of the weather itself – 'light – dews – breezes – bloom – and freshness'. When the *Morning Post* praised his picture of *Englefield House*, exhibited at the Royal Academy in 1833, Shee[1] said rather tartly that 'it was only a picture of a house, and ought to have been put in the Architectural Room'. 'I told him,' reports the artist, 'it was a picture of a summer morning, *including a house*.' As for the more exotic romanticism of Turner, Sir George could never come to terms with it; he complained of its bravura and 'false taste' and thought he had done harm 'by endeavouring to make painting in oil to appear like watercolours, by which attempting to give lightness and clearness the force of oil painting has been lost'.

It was long before Sir George could recognize that Constable, although a landscape painter, was an artist of a wholly different kind from himself. He lent him his pictures to copy, invited him to his house, was solicitous for his health, and gave him well-meant advice. But only the last years of their friendship showed the patron-artist relationship at its best and most fruitful – years in which Beaumont's own pictures began to move away from his earlier style and to show a delight in the real and familiar world of England, as in some of his last studies of landscapes near Coleorton.

[1] Sir Martin Arthur Shee (1769–1850), portrait painter, who succeeded Lawrence as P.R.A. in 1830.

In 1823 Constable was invited to visit the Beaumonts in their Leicestershire home, and went there with some reluctance, not wishing 'to witness the rotting, melancholy dissolution of the trees which two months ago were so beautiful'. But once arrived, he wrote to his wife in a glow of enthusiasm. House and garden delighted him – 'such grounds, such trees, such distances'; he was intoxicated by the pictures all around him, the Claudes, the Cozens, the Swaneveldt in the breakfast room, on which the sun glowed as it set, the portfolios of drawings, the books, all so lavishly at his disposal; and most of all he was charmed, as so many guests before him, with his host and hostess themselves. The warm, happy house comes alive in his letters – Lady Beaumont with her quick enthusiastic speech, her lively sensibility, reading Wordsworth's poetry in the light of many candles, or Sir George declaiming Shakespeare, while the guest turns over the prints and drawings with which they have provided him; Sir George's serenity and liveliness, and dry, ironic wit; a happy evening shared with Southey and his wife and daughter who were also staying in the house; Sir George's sixty-ninth birthday, celebrated by a servant's ball, when Constable was lulled to sleep by a fiddle; the ordered piety of family prayers at the Hall and Sunday observance at the little church where Beaumont ancestors slept in their marble tomb; above all the hours and hours with Sir George in painting-room or garden. Here occurred those conversations which Leslie, a little jealous of Beaumont, recounted as if to show the patron's conventional blindness, but which surely show a readiness to exchange ideas and to learn from originality. Wilkie lacked either the ability or the temerity to question Sir George's judgment. He wrote to his patron with admiration for one of his pictures possessed by the actor, Bannister, and praises in particular 'the clear and juicy brown of the trees and ground'. But Constable, for whom spring was the painter's season, whose subjects were light and warmth and the freshness of a just departed shower, taught him to look with new eyes. When

Sir George wanted to match his own painting to the tints of a Gaspar Poussin, Constable exclaimed that if Poussin were to rise from the grave he could hardly know his own picture, darkened with dirt and age. When Beaumont suggested the colour of an old Cremona fiddle for the prevailing tone of a painting, Constable laid a fiddle on the green lawn before the house. And, in a well-worn anecdote, when Beaumont asked whether it were not difficult to decide the placing of his 'brown tree', Constable cheerfully replied: 'Not in the least, for I never put such a thing into a picture.' The bluntness and vigour of the younger man's rejoinders suggest the give and take of men on equal ground, concerned to find the truth rather than perpetuate tradition; and Sir George's later paintings show how much he finally learned from the greater artist's precept and example.

This was the visit which concluded with the noble painting made 'in the dark recesses of the garden', where the lime trees were now grown tall above the Reynolds cenotaph. It was to be exhibited years after Sir George Beaumont's death, and the autumnal tints seem a premonition of elegy.

CHAPTER VIII

Interchange of Knowledge and Delight

Those who enjoyed the Beaumonts' patronage enjoyed their friendship also. This was the gift that charmed so many, the unaffected warmth of heart which made social distinctions wholly irrelevant; and nowhere is it more apparent than in the rich relationship between them, Coleridge, and the Wordsworths.

It was a meeting of minds and hearts which might well have astonished anyone who knew the two poets in their early manhood, when both were professed democrats. Coleridge's early letters are full of passionate declamations against the rich.

It is our pestilent Commerce, our unnatural Crowding together of men in Cities, and our Government by Rich Men, that are bringing about the manifestations of offended Deity.

The Country is divided into two Classes – one rioting and wallowing in the wantonness of wealth, the other struggling for the necessaries of Life. . . . It is necessary for the human Being in the present state of society to have felt the pressures of actual Hardships, in order to be a moral Being. Where these have been never and in no degree felt, our very deeds of Pity do to a certain point co-operate to deprave us. Consider for a moment the different Feelings with which a poor woman in a cottage gives a piece of Bread and a cup of warm Tea to another poor Woman travelling with a Babe at her Back, and the Feelings with which a Lady lets two pence drop from her Carriage Window, out of the envelope of perfumed Paper by which her Pocket is defended from the Pollution of Copper – the difference is endless.

The chief theme of Wordsworth's earlier poetry is that 'bad is the world and hard is the world's law', and he was even more emphatic than Coleridge about 'the insolence and presumption of the aristocracy'. Coleridge excused it at least in part by the isolation from the poorer people which wealth imposed; but his friend had been embittered by a long lawsuit to recover his small patrimony from the money owed to his father by the first Earl of Lonsdale – a man of very different character from his successor, who was to be a good friend to the poet. Wordsworth was convinced that 'hereditary distinctions and privileged orders of every species must necessarily counteract the progress of human improvement'. In the early days of their friendship both still believed that political action might help to relieve hardship and social injustice. They dallied with revolutionary enthusiasm abroad and democratic movements at home, even arousing government suspicion by their hospitality to the republican Thelwall soon after his release from prison; but even the government was unable to take them seriously as spies, and despite their indiscretions they went unharmed. But it was not long before they lost faith in overt political action; they were patriots and democrats, not revolutionaries. They both abhorred violence, and feared the excesses of a possible revolution as keenly as any Tory in the country, and they were soon disillusioned by personal knowledge of some of the radical leaders.

The professed Democrats (Coleridge writes bitterly to Thomas Poole in 1801), who on an occasion of uproar would press forward to be the Leaders, are without knowledge, talents, or morals. I have conversed with the most celebrated among them; more gross, ignorant, and perverted men I never wish to see again! – O it would have made you, my friend! 'a sadder and a wiser man' if you had been with me at one of Horne Tooke's public Dinners! – I could never discover by any train of Questions that any of these Lovers of Liberty had either [a] distinct *object* for their Wishes, or distinct views of the *means*.

Men of imagination, more sensitive than most to 'the still, sad music of humanity', are bound to feel passionately about socials evils; they are equally bound in time to reject the inadequacy and limitation of political action and to realize that only an awakened imagination can rouse men to real caring for their fellows. The two friends remained republicans at heart for many years, and even as late as 1809 Beaumont solemnly cautioned young Haydon against Wordsworth's 'terrific democratic notions'; but their weapons now became those of the imagination, of poetry which reveals the ordinary affections of ordinary men as things of infinite worth, their endurance of common ills and their daily sympathies with each other as matter of sublimity. One of the most 'political' actions of Wordsworth's life was his dedication of his 1801 volume of poems to Charles James Fox, that great-hearted man whose warmth and kindliness attached men's devotion, whatever his private faults.

. . . Being utterly unknown to you as I am, I am well aware, that if I am justified in writing to you at all, it is necessary, my letter should be short; but I have feelings within me which I hope will so far show themselves in this Letter as to excuse the trespass which I am afraid I shall make. In common with the whole of the English People I have observed in your public character a constant predominance of sensibility of heart. Necessitated as you have been from your public situation to have much to do with men in bodies, and in classes, and accordingly to contemplate them in that relation, it has been your praise that you have not thereby been prevented from looking upon them as individuals, and that you have habitually left your heart open to be influenced by them in that capacity. This habit cannot but have made you dear to Poets; and I am sure that, if since your first entrance into public life there has been a single true poet living in England, he must have loved you.
. . . It appears to me that the most calamitous effect, which has followed the measures which have lately been pursued in this country, is a rapid decay of the domestic affections among the lower orders of society. This effect the present Rulers of this Country are not conscious of, or they disregard it. For many years past, the tendency of society amongst almost all the nations of Europe has been to produce it. But recently by the spreading of manufactures through every part of the country, by the heavy taxes

upon postage, by workhouses, Houses of Industry, and the invention of Soup-shops &c &c superadded to the increasing disproportion between the price of labour and that of the necessaries of life, the bonds of domestic feeling among the poor, as far as the influence of these things has extended, have been weakened, and in innumerable instances entirely destroyed. The evil would be the less to be regretted, if these institutions were regarded only as palliatives to a disease; but the vanity and pride of their promoters are so subtly interwoven with them, that they are deemed great discoveries and blessings to humanity. In the meantime parents are separated from their children, and children from their parents; the wife no longer prepares with her own hands a meal for her husband, the produce of his labour; there is little doing in his house in which his affections can be interested, and but little left in it which he can love.

. . . In the two poems, *The Brothers* and *Michael*, I have attempted to draw a picture of the domestic affections as I know they exist amongst a class of men who are now almost confined to the North of England. They are small independent *proprietors* of land here called statesmen, men of respectable education who daily labour on their own little properties. The domestic affections will always be strong amongst men who live in a country not crowded with population, if these men are placed above poverty. But if they are the proprietors of small estates, which have descended to them from their ancestors, the power which these affections will acquire amongst such men is inconceivable, by those who have only had an opportunity of observing hired labourers, farmers, and the manufacturing Poor. Their little tract of land serves as a kind of permanent rallying point for their domestic feelings, as a tablet upon which they are written which makes them objects of memory in a thousand instances when they would otherwise be forgotten. It is a fountain fitted to the nature of social man from which supplies of affection, as pure as his heart was intended for, are daily drawn. This class of men is rapidly disappearing. You, Sir, have a consciousness, upon which every good man will congratulate you, that the whole of your public conduct has in one way or other been directed to the preservation of this class of men, and those who hold similar situations. You have felt that the most sacred of all property is the property of the Poor. The two Poems which I have mentioned were written with a view to show that men who do not wear fine

cloaths can feel deeply. . . . [They] may in some small degree
enlarge our feelings of reverence for our species, and our knowledge
of human nature, by shewing that our best qualities are possessed
by men whom we are too apt to consider, not with reference to the
points in which they resemble us, but to those in which they mani-
festly differ from us. I thought, at a time when these feelings are
sapped in so many ways that the two poems might co-operate,
however feebly, with the illustrious efforts which you have made to
stem this and other evils with which the country is labouring, and it
is on this account alone that I have taken the liberty of thus ad-
dressing you.

Such was the professed 'democracy' of both poets when in
the spring of 1803 Coleridge had his first inauspicious meeting
with Sir George Beaumont. They met by chance at dinner, as
fellow guests at Sotheby's house in London, and Sir George
took an instant dislike to this plump, enthusiastic, talkative
young man, far too flamboyant for one of his own courteously
schooled and slightly ironic disposition. He merely 'considered
how he should shun him' in the future. He had almost forgotten him by the summer of that same year when he leased
part of William Jackson's Keswick property, Greta Hall, for
a long painting holiday, only to discover that the other part
of the same house was leased by Coleridge. In an enforced
neighbourliness, removed from all the restless contacts of his
own London circle, and compelled to see his volatile acquaintance frequently and at leisure, Sir George soon revised his
first impression, and both he and his wife recognized in him
not only a genius but a man capable of intense unselfish
devotion. Self-*centred* indeed he was, but generous in admiration, always quick to prefer his friends in honour and esteem.
This was the quality, so akin to his own, which won Beaumont's
heart. He later told Farington of his 'good fortune in having
met such a genius as Coleridge, and a man of such disposition
that He would to go the end of the world to serve another;
that Wordsworth, not himself, was his Theme, His friendship
being above all self-love'. Characteristically, Coleridge's

[107]

first thought was to introduce his new friends to the Wordsworths. Sir George was amiably willing, Lady Beaumont
eager for such a meeting. Although she welcomed Coleridge
always with most solicitous kindness, and even thought of
him at times as a spiritual adviser, she stood a little in awe of
his metaphysical fireworks, his range of knowledge and speed
of thought. Now, persuaded by this rather alarming young
man to read his friend's poetry, she found in it the simplicity,
the sensibility, the warmth and steady strength of feeling
that reflected her own heart. Coleridge writes delightedly
to Wordsworth;

Sir G. & Lady B. are half-mad to see you – (Lady B. told me, that
the night before last as she was reading your Poem on Cape
RASH JUDGMENT, had you entered the room, she believes she should
have fallen at your feet) Sir G. & his wife both say, that the Picture
gives them an idea of you as a profound strong-minded Philosopher, not as a Poet – I answered (& I believe, truly) that so it
must needs do, if it were a good Portrait – for that you were a great
Poet by inspirations, & in the Moments of revelation, but that you
were a thinking feeling Philosopher habitually – that your Poetry
was your Philosophy under the action of strong winds of Feeling –
a sea rolling high.

(The poem is that beginning 'A narrow girdle of rough
stones and crags', composed and published in 1800.) What
poet would not respond to such a reader, the friend of such
a friend? It was fortunate that the Beaumonts, in their first
acquaintance with Wordsworth's poetry, had his finest and
most sensitive interpreter at hand. Wordsworth must have
been all the more moved that it was this particular poem
which Margaret Beaumont chose to admire so much, for it
is a microcosm of all that he intended in his work. Modern
readers are rarely familiar with it, although it bears much
the same relation to *Resolution and Independence* as one of
Constable's watercolour studies to the finished painting.
Wordsworth, his sister, and Coleridge are straying idly along

the eastern shore of Grasmere in the sun-thinned mist of a September morning, noting with loving particularity 'feather, or leaf, or weed, or withered bough', watching dandelion or thistledown 'that skimmed the surface of the dead calm lake', and listening to the talk and laughter of the reapers in a nearby field. The sense of happy relaxation, of the gaiety of friends, the privilege of idleness, lulls the reader like the late summer warmth. Then suddenly they see 'through a thin veil of glittering haze'

> *on a point of jutting land,*
> *The tall and upright figure of a Man*
> *Attired in peasant's garb, who stood alone,*
> *Angling beside the margin of the lake.*

We experience the momentary shock of vision which all Wordsworth's solitary figures induce in a reader. Here is a man sharply distinct from the natural scene, yet part of it; there is an Aeschylean quality in his isolation, as if he is set apart by endurance or contemplation, yet he has the inevitability, the rightness, of a boulder or a cloud, at one with the landscape itself. Then the moment of vision passes, the gleam in the mind goes out. This is just an idle peasant, throwing away a day's earnings; *he* has no privilige to be idle. They draw near, and the fisherman turns his head to greet them. A gaunt, grey face, legs so long and thin they seem scarcely able to hold up the emaciated frame – not an idler, but a man too starved and sick to labour, hoping only for a miserable alms from 'the dead unfeeling lake'! His uncomplaining existence reproaches their rash judgment, as it reproaches human charity and the whole social system which sanctions idle comfort (however frugal) on one hand and despairing poverty on the other.

> *The happy idleness of that sweet morn,*
> *With all its lovely images, was changed.*

In the trivial episode, perceived with an intensity of moral feeling that gives it dignity and power, Margaret Beaumont could recognize a spirit that felt like hers but with greater strength and keener consciousness. There is nothing mawkish or exaggerated in the admiration she expresses with the uninhibited sentiment of her period. Burke and Fox, after all, had been known to weep openly in the House of Commons when a rift occurred between them; while the Duke of Newcastle, assuming office, sobbed in the king's presence with an abandon that would have made Lord Lundy envious. The modern world, as dully monotonous in its sentiments as in its clothes, finds it hard to understand that romantic sensibility is not insincerity. So, fully prepared for mutual admiration, the Beaumonts and the Wordsworths met. There is no record of this first encounter, though judging by Wordsworth's first letter to them that autumn it must have been brief and formal.

It is a very remarkable letter, both in substance and tone. At some point, before or after this first meeting, Beaumont had made a characteristic gesture. Enthralled by his new friends, impressed by the closeness of their relationship, perceptive enough to realize how much each owed to the stimulus of the other, he conceived a plan to make them close and permanent neighbours. He bought a small property at Applethwaite, close to Keswick, and presented it to Wordsworth so that the two men of genius might live always near each other. But with his usual delicacy and regard for feeling, he hesitated at offering officious kindness to his new acquaintance, and asked Coleridge himself to hand over the deeds and explain the situation. Wordsworth was so overcome that he allowed eight weeks to elapse before writing an acknowledgment, and then excused himself as restrained by the nervous excitement and illness which, he claimed, was induced by writing. But probably he was held back chiefly by diffidence at so generous and unlooked for a gift, combined with his realization that by the time he could build on Applethwaite the volatile Coleridge would have gone, for he was already considering a more equable climate for the benefit of his health. He tried to explain, and suggested that he might perhaps be regarded as a temporary steward of the new estate. His tone was stiff, formal, and slightly embarrassed; yet he included, chiefly for Lady Beaumont, his sister's transcript of two or three of his poems, and is composed enough to add gossip about the local militia. The inhabitants of Grasmere 'have turned out almost to a man. We are to go to Ambleside on Sunday to be mustered, and to put on, for the first time, our military apparel.' (Wordsworth in the militia is an awe-inspiring thought.)

The difference in tone in letters passing between the Beaumonts, the Wordsworths, and Coleridge, makes an interesting study in human relationships. Coleridge's letters from the first are voluble, enthusiastic, generous, with that almost pathetic eagerness to please and to be loved that characterized so many of his relationships. He has no reserves; 'it is among my wishes to write my whole life to you', he confesses within six months of the Keswick meeting. His illness and pain, his haunted, sleepless nights, his past convictions and his present beliefs, his devotion to his new friends, all pour out in a rapid frothing stream. His first parting from them is a grief, as he gazes at one of Sir George's sketches in the hollow quietness that, despite continuing sound, seems always to possess a house when friends have gone. 'It will give a lasting interest to the Drawing of the Waterfall that I first saw it through tears.' The little fat baby Derwent, who always seemed much more stolid than his sensitive, brilliant, elder brother, Hartley, also resented their going.

Poor little Derwent has been in such a crowd, that he did not seem to know that you were gone, till this afternoon, when we had the house to ourselves. Then he went to your room, and he has been crying piteously, 'Lady Beaumont's gone away, & I WILL be a naughty boy; Lady Beaumont's gone away'.

One is reminded sadly that the woman who could so attach the heart of a little boy was herself childless. Very soon Coleridge feels at home enough with his new friends to suggest a series of poetical 'translations' from some of Beaumont's drawings, and gets as far as planning whether each shall be 'a moral-descriptive poem, whether an inscription, whether a tale' – another project that apparently came to nothing, despite the Polonius-solemnity of its inception. He must, he says, write to them as old friends or not at all.

Wordsworth's earlier letters are in a different tone. He began almost at a disadvantage, as the Applethwaite property must have bred a sense of obligation, however little intended. There is more dignity and reserve in his first letters, even a little stiffness. Yet, outside the small circle of his family and Coleridge, his feeling for the Beaumonts was to become probably the most profound of all his affections, with the quiet strength and depth and tenacity which marked the few intense loves of his life. It grew more slowly than Coleridge's, but he is able to write in 1806:

'It is indeed a great happiness to me to be beloved by you, and to think upon what foundation that love rests . . . I esteem your friendship one of the best gifts of my life.'

As for Lady Beaumont and Dorothy they achieved an easy simplicity of affection quite different in kind from that of their men. They write to each other as equals, of the ordinary feminine interests of house and children and neighbours and, of course, of the common concern of both for the health and spirits of Wordsworth and Sir George.

Hazlitt too might have been among the Beaumonts' new friends in Cumberland, were it not for his own unhappy disposition. He was no longer the hero-worshipping youngster who had walked in a dream of glory from Shropshire to Somerset in order to visit Coleridge. Dark, brooding, spiky as a porcupine from the America of his own infancy, he was invited to dine with Coleridge at the Beaumonts' table. Always interested in a young artist, Sir George was gracious until the unfortunate moment when Coleridge began an attack on Junius, the polemical Whig who had so brilliantly satirized the government of some thirty years before. Hazlitt at once and ardently defended him, partly on principle as a genuine admirer of his talents, partly because Coleridge was toppling from his earlier pedestal, partly from his demon of sheer contrariness, partly perhaps because he a little resented his elegant and wealthy host even while hoping for a commission from him. A fierce dispute ensued and the party broke up in an uncomfortable atmosphere. Next day Coleridge called upon Hazlitt with his own interlined copy of Junius 'full of expressions of admiration', and urging him to realize 'how foolish it is for persons who respect each other to dispute warmly, for after all they probably think the same'. But the damage was done. Hazlitt was sulky and Sir George offended. His young guest had unpardonably forgotten himself, had supported a damnable Whig at the very table of his Tory host, in terms too heated for civility, and in disrespectful argument with his host's respected friend. Hazlitt complained years later that 'in disgust he never saw me afterwards, and I lost the expectation of gaining a patron'. But Sir George was fair-minded enough still to commission from him portraits of Wordsworth and Coleridge as he had originally intended.

Meanwhile it became clear that Wordsworth was never to live at Applethwaite as Beaumont had hoped when making the gift, for there was no longer any reason in such a move. Coleridge's health was declining rapidly and he was now resolved to seek a cure in living abroad. He obtained a minor government post at Malta, and set off to London to make his preparations in the spring of 1804. At once Sir George met him with kindnesses, advised him on his needs, and gave him an introduction to Richard Payne Knight[1] so that he might see

---

[1] Richard Payne Knight (1750–1824), collector of bronzes, coins, and gems, and writer on landscape gardening. He bequeathed his immensely valuable collection to the British Museum.

the latter's magnificent collection of bronzes. Then when all seemed ready, he swept him off to Dunmow to rest before his final departure, where he was welcomed by both, as Coleridge wrote to his wife, with 'glowing affection'. They were indeed as good to him as if he had been a son. 'I was welcomed *almost* as you welcomed me at Racedown,' he wrote to the Wordsworths, 'and their solicitude of affection is enough to effeminate one.' With his insatiable need to be loved, he adored every fresh evidence of their care for him.

My spirit watched as constantly and as shyly the numberless kind attentions of Sir George and Lady Beaumont, as an innocent young woman pleased and uncoy, the intelligible all of a lover's behaviour.

Soothed and cherished, he relaxed, happy to learn of pictures and painters from his host, to exchange reflections on religion with his hostess, with whose quiet faith both he and Wordsworth had much in common, to discuss with Sir George the possibility of finding a drawing-master at Keswick for little Hartley, who showed promise, and to ride for the sake of the exercise – almost inevitably being thrown off, while crossing Lord Maynard's park. He had learned little about horsemanship from his brief experience as a trooper. When at last he returned to London, Dorothy Wordsworth wrote to him regretfully:

I am sorry you have left Dunmow, because the Beaumonts are so good and kind-hearted that I think you must there have had home feelings about you, something like being among us.

But the boat was not yet ready to leave, and in a few days Coleridge was again staying with his kind friends, this time in the house at Grosvenor Square. While there he was as free to welcome his other friends as if he were in his own home; and among them he presented the Cornishman, Humphry Davy, already well known as a progressive young scientist, and later a frequent caller at the Beaumonts. Davy wished to pay a farewell visit, but was diffident because he could only come late in the evening, until Coleridge encouraged him.

Of course I shall see you this evening here at a quarter after nine. When I mentioned it to Sir George, 'Too late,' said he; 'no, if it were twelve o'clock, it would be better than his not coming.' Sir George is a remarkably *sensible* man which I mention because it *is* somewhat REMARKABLE in a painter of genius, who is at the same time a man of rank and an exceedingly amusing companion.

At last the parting came. Coleridge wrote to Southey from Portsmouth, urging him to call on the Beaumonts, who 'are worth going a good way to see for their own sakes', and who will give letters of introduction so that he may see some of the famous private collections of art. He goes on to describe his leave-taking from his hosts.

It would have affected you deeply to have seen the manner in which Sir George parted from me. – His Valet packed up everything – sent off everything, & did not leave me till I entered the Mail. – They stocked me with Wines in stout bottles & lock-up cases, with Medicine, Portable Soup, an elegant Thing to lock up my Letters, Papers, &c &c – & when I was at Dunmow, Sir George thrice entreated me to accept of an £100 – the which I mildly but firmly refused/but on the morning I left Dunmow, as I was going into the Coach, the Servant delivered me a Letter from Sir George, with the £100 inclosed – & the Letter itself for its delicacy, deliberate Affection, and elevated good sense was 'worth twice the sum', to use a very vulgar phrase.

Lady Beaumont's parting gift was an Italian grammar and dictionary, 'as portable as could be carried', and with this he passed from the sight and largely from the knowledge of his friends for the next two years.

Meanwhile the Wordsworths' intimacy with the Beaumonts developed into the warmest friendship, very largely through the unsophisticated affection between Dorothy and Margaret Beaumont. Lady Beaumont sent parcels of books for the children (she was godmother to one of them), was interested in their childish ailments, contributed to the small acts of kindness that Dorothy out of her own straitened means tried to perform for her neighbours in times of stress. The spontaneous happiness with which Dorothy writes of the birth of William's second son is characteristic of their letters.

Grasmere, Tuesday evening, June 17th.

My dear Friend, – You will rejoice with us in my sister's safety, and the birth of a son. There was something peculiarly affecting to us in the time and manner of this child's coming into the world. It was like the very same thing over again that happened three years ago; for on the 18th of June, on such another morning, after such a clear and starlight night, the birds singing in the orchard in full assembly as on this 15th, the young swallows chirping in the self-same nest at the chamber window, the rose-trees rich with roses in the garden, the sun shining on the mountains, the air still and balmy, on such a morning was Johnny born, and all our first feelings were revived at the birth of his brother two hours later in the day, and three days earlier in the month; and I fancied that I felt a double rushing-in of love for it, when I saw the child, as if I had both what had been the first-born infant John's share of love to give it, and its own.

Wordsworth too writes with the humour that so often delighted his friends, rather to the surprise of those who know only his poetry. He gives a lively account of the two young men who have taken a summer cottage at Grasmere, one pale and interesting, the other painted, straying modishly with their lapdog along the country lanes, startling the sober inhabitants with their 'green leather caps, turkey half-boots, jackets of fine linen, or long dressing-gowns, as suit them'. But one person at least lamented when they departed.

The Vale is relieved of our harlequins, to the great loss of my daughter, who had conceived a great attachment for them and their doggy.

The Beaumonts must especially have welcomed this particular letter as a sign that Wordsworth was at least emerging
from the paralysing effect of the death of his brother John,
drowned off Weymouth in the spring of 1805 while in command of the East Indiaman, the *Abergavenny*. Their separated
and unhappy childhood had given both William and Dorothy
an unusually strong sense of family so that the grief and shock
of this event was proportionately stronger. Wordsworth had
found it impossible to ease his heart in elegy, but instead had
worked grimly on at *The Prelude*. The long autobiographical
poem helped him in some sense to reintegrate his life, but
he had finished it in June with no sense of comfort.

I was dejected on many accounts: when I looked back upon the
performance, it seemed to have a dead weight about it – the reality
so far short of the expectation. It was the first long labour that I had
finished; and the doubt whether I should ever live to write The
Recluse, and the sense which I had of this poem being so far below
what I seemed capable of executing, depressed me much; above all,
many heavy thoughts of my poor departed brother hung upon me,
the joy which I should have had in showing him the manuscript,
and a thousand other vain fancies and dreams.

None the less, writing *The Prelude* had been more therapeutic
than he realized. At last he could face steadily the reality of
loss, and one of Sir George's own pictures proved a means
of healing. *Peele Castle in a Storm* is a characteristic piece of
romantic painting, undoubtedly inspired by Cozens' painting
of the coast between Vietri and Salerno. It is a dark and rather
heavy picture, in which the ruined castle on its crag almost
merges with the swirling sky, while just below an area of
storm-light a small boat tosses perilously upon an angry sea.
Unlike the Cozens, it is a carefully composed exercise in the
sublime, but the subject spoke straight to Wordsworth's
heart. Grief for his brother and love for the painter were
suddenly identified in a moment of cathartic vision. He could
at last break from the chrysalis in which he had been frozen

all the spring, look back with clearer eyes at the illusory images of untroubled calm which he had earlier taken for truth, and find new strength and endurance in the very power of tempest, 'this sea in anger and that dismal shore'. (Constable was to quote the same line some years later as an epigraph to his own painting of Weymouth Bay, in which the wreck of a small boat tosses in the waves, perhaps as a reference to the loss of the *Abergavenny*.)

William and Dorothy looked back upon that spring and summer as 'a dreary dream'. Their grief was too raw to be much spoken of between them; from Coleridge, whose return was now expected, there was no direct news; no one knew quite where he was, though there were rumours that all his papers and possessions had been lost at sea; moreover the house at Grasmere was cramped and inconvenient for the growing family. Again the Beaumonts' thoughtfulness eased their troubles. The rebuilding of Coleorton was nearly completed, and meanwhile the owners lived in the London house. But the farmhouse near the new hall was empty for the time: their friends would indeed do them a kindness by spending the winter there until they could find better accommodation in their own country. They could keep an eye on the progress of the building; and Wordsworth, who had written so delightfully about the design of the new gardens, might even be prevailed upon to plan a winter garden there himself. So gracious and kindly an inspiration worked the cure that was intended. By the autumn of 1806, Wordsworth and his wife, Dorothy, and the children, were all installed at the farmhouse at Coleorton.

They were delighted by everything, the roominess of the house, the flaming autumn sunsets above the flat fields of Leicestershire – new to those whose skies were so often shut away by mountains – the walks in Charnwood and especially to Grace Dieu, even though the road to Ashby-de-la-Zouche itself was so bad that 'the Ashby people think we are marvellous to wade through it'. Little Johnny, too, is thrilled with a new home from which he goes to school for the first time. Not quite four years old, 'he goes with his dinner in a bag slung over his shoulder, and a little bottle of milk in his greatcoat pocket, and never man was fuller of pride and self-importance'. The neighbours were mildly surprised by young women who insisted on walking so much under conditions that would have shocked Jane Austen's Misses Bingley; the Scots gardener, Craig (who delighted his fellow-countryman, Wilkie), was civil but suspicious of Wordsworth's gardening; old Mitchell, the night-watchman, told him lengthy and circumstantial stories of the local ghosts; while an aged labourer was so fascinated by the poet's habit of composing aloud as he tramped up and down the garden walks that he followed behind, getting whole verses by heart. The northern visitors were undoubtedly oddities to the locals, but they were simple and good-hearted enough to find acceptance.

Coleridge returned to England, and after many delays joined his friends at Coleorton in the week before Christmas. Sitting by the farmhouse fire, amid 'that happy vision of beloved faces', watched by Dorothy's quick and loving solicitude, he listened as Wordsworth read *The Prelude* – a time of such intimacy and restored happiness that he celebrated it in poetry before he slept as

> *A tale of high and passionate thoughts*
> *To their own music chanted.*

His response shows that remarkable intuition into the true nature of his friends' work, which moves us by its sensitive sympathy as much as the rest of his poem by its self-distrust yet generous praise of another man's achievement.

Coleridge came and went, and in the following summer Wordsworth and his wife went up to London, returning in the autumn with Sir Walter Scott, who is reputed to have planned the tournament scenes of *Ivanhoe* while sitting in a little stone arbour in Wordsworth's new winter garden. Under the influence of renewed happiness, fresh scenes and interests, Wordsworth found himself able at last to write again as freely as before John's death. (The *Song at the Feast of Brougham Castle*, written during this period, is dedicated to Beaumont's friend, Lord Lonsdale; and Sir George's influence may have helped to reconcile Wordsworth to the Lowther family, as well as the repayment of the money owed to his father by the previous earl.)

The long sojourn at Coleorton confirmed the equality of friendship between the Wordsworths and the Beaumonts. Never again can Wordsworth write, as he had once done, with the slight reserve of a man of genius to a patron. Their friendship is close enough to remove even the invisible barrier of wealth. Dorothy accepts without embarrassment that Lady Beaumont can afford to frank their correspondence better than she can; and some years later when Sir George wishes to contribute to the expenses of John's university career, Wordsworth accepts his gift with gratitude and common-sense.

We sacrifice our time, our ease, and often our health, for the sake of our friends. . . . I will not then pay *money* such a compliment as to allow *it* to be too precious a thing to be added to the catalogue where fortunes are unequal, and where the occasion is deemed mutually important.

Both men respect each other as practitioners in different arts. The poet is at times inspired by the painter's pictures, as when one of Sir George's views of Coleorton move him to lines which so oddly anticipate Keat's *Ode on a Grecian Urn*.

> *Praised be the Art whose subtle power could stay*
> *Yon cloud, and fix it in that glorious shape;*
> *Nor would permit the thin smoke to escape,*
> *Nor those bright sunbeams to forsake the day;*
> *Which stopped that band of travellers on their way,*
> *Ere they were lost within the shady wood;*
> *And showed the Bark upon the glassy flood*

For ever anchored in her sheltering bay,
Soul-soothing Art! whom Morning, Noontide, Even,
Do serve with all their changeful pageantary;
Thou, with ambition modest yet sublime,
Here, for the sight of mortal man, hast given
To one brief moment caught from fleeting time
The appropriate calm of blest eternity.

But it was a mutual relationship.

One wooed the silent Art with studious pains:
These groves have heard the Other's pensive strains;
Devoted thus, their spirits did unite
By interchange of knowledge and delight.

The poet admires the painter but is just as ready to instruct him in the principles of poetic taste. Most of Sir George's friends listened respectfully to his advice, whether they intended to follow it or not. Wordsworth was the only one who at all times assumed that in his own art *he* was the authority. 'I wish to be considered as a teacher or nothing,' he once wrote to Beaumont about the intention of his own verse. He found indeed a ready discipleship, especially in Lady Beaumont, whose likeness to Dorothy was more than once remarked. She 'verily has a soul', wrote Coleridge, 'in point of quick enthusiastic Feeling, most like to Dorothy's – only not Dorothy's powers'; and Wordsworth instructed her as if she too were his sister. He was fond of quoting Coleridge's dictum that every new and original writer must himself create the taste by which he is to be relished, but in her gentle, reflective, religious nature that taste was already half formed. 'To be incapable of a feeling for poetry, in my sense of the word,' he wrote to her, 'is to be without love of human nature and reverence for God.' She was more able than anyone, outside his own family and Coleridge, to understand the odd paradox of his disinterested love for man and his own introspective self-absorption; which was after all no paradox, because what he loved in men was not their variety but the basic fact of their humanity itself, the power to love and to endure, even in the humblest lives: and this he could best study in that which was nearest to him, his own heart. Like Dorothy, too, she had that quick perception of natural detail which she could share with a mind more powerful than her own. There are two brief, illuminating entries in Coleridge's notebook just before his voyage to Malta.

The Water lily in the midst of the Lake is equally refreshed by the Rain, as the Spurge on the sandy Shore.

And again:

The water-lily=spurge – L. Beaumont.

One is reminded of Dorothy's single red leaf that dances for ever in *Christabel*.

Both the Beaumonts could respond readily to the religious and reflective qualities of romantic poetry. Lady Beaumont told Coleridge how, as a child, she would endeavour 'to think of a mountain, or great River, or something *great*, in order to raise up her Soul and kindle it', before saying her prayers; while Sir George confided to Farington that 'he was infinitely indebted to Wordsworth for the good he had received from His poetry which had benefited Him more, Had more purified His mind, that any Sermons had done'. But it was she who understood most fully how much he intended in the simple, natural images of his lyric poems, and who was able to share her pleasure in them with her favourite sister, Mrs Frances Fermor. Wordsworth rejoiced to hear that Mrs Fermor had singled out his *Daffodils* and *The Rock Crowned with Snowdrops*. 'Whoever is much pleased with either of these quiet and tender delineations must be fitted to walk through the recesses of my poetry with delight.'

They did more than walk through it with delight. They

insisted that their friends should do so too. In season and out of season they championed their friend's work, even when it was least popular with the critics. Lady Beaumont read his poems to those who stayed under her roof, or pressed the volume upon them with an enthusiasm hard to resist, while Sir George tried to explain the principles upon which they were written. His verbal echoes of the critical dicta of Wordsworth and Coleridge reveal how often these matters must have been discussed between them. He defended Wordsworth to Farington against the attacks of the Edinburgh reviewers almost in Coleridge's words.

[He] said that all men who write in a new & superior stile must *create a people capable* of fully relishing their beauties, & that at present, prejudice and an established habit of admiring certain works prevents the works of Wordsworth from being duly appreciated.

The 'established habit' of tastes formed in their own youth were now rejected, and they learned to disapprove the style of Johnson and Pope, although Sir George's repudiation of them was a little more cautious than his wife's. Lady Beaumont indeed reminds one strongly of Marianne Dashwood in *Sense and Sensibility*, ascertaining that her young man is suitably devoted to Cowper and admires Pope no more than is proper. By such discussions among their wide circle of acquaintance, and such repeated praise, they did much to open the way for a more general acceptance of the new poetry. How well they learned Wordsworthian principles of taste and encouraged them in others appears in one of Sir George's letters to Lady Mulgrave in 1811. He is assured by her renewed delight in nature of her return to perfect health.

Your delightful enthusiasm shews that you now not only see the lovely scenes around you, but feel how beautiful they are. – The sun is confessedly a glorious object, when he only dazzles the eyes; but when we feel him shine warmly upon our hearts – we may be

sure all is well – in my mind there cannot be a stronger proof of
health and vigour than a pregnant & inward relish of the exquisite
charms of nature.

In another and very practical way the patron served the poet
with the best means he had, showing his approval to the
world at large by contributing three engravings from his
own pictures to the 1815 edition of Wordsworth's poems,
as illustrations to *Lucy Gray, Peele Castle, and Peter Bell*;
and receiving in return the author's dedication of the volume.

In later years, during the long, miserable estrangement
between the poets, they both continued to write to the
Beaumonts, who tried still to befriend them with equal
solicitude. But faithful though they both were, it is clear
that Wordsworth was the dearer friend. Lady Beaumont supported Coleridge's public lectures, helped to make them
known, and was active in gaining further support for them.
His election to the Royal Society of Literature, with the
pension consequent upon it, owed something to Sir George's
friendship with the Hon George Agar Ellis, one of the
Society's first vice-presidents; and Beaumont even tried – un-
successfully – to persuade Kemble to present Coleridge's
Osorio at Covent Garden. Coleridge loved them still, but
was sometimes suspicious and irritable as his maladies grew
upon him, demanding, as the hypersensitive are apt to do,
even more attention than they could give. The tone of his
letters to them and about them varies from devoted attachment to carping criticism. Perhaps Lady Beaumont tried him
rather far when in 1814 she enlisted his help for her sister,
Mrs Fermor. This lady, whose husband was a distant connection of that Arabella Fermor whose outraged dignity had
occasioned Pope's *Rape of the Lock*, seems to have had her
sister's sensibility with less of her charm. As she grew older
she became a prey to the nervous depression which darkened
so many of her contemporaries, and Margaret Beaumont persuaded her to go to Bristol to have the advantage of Cole-

ridge's spiritual advice – remembering no doubt those reflective religious conversations of her own early friendship
with him. But Coleridge was too spent himself to give such
help to others, and perhaps he was right in attributing the
lady's trouble partly to physical causes. In that period of
enormous meals, when dinner rarely took less than two hours,
some of the prevailing 'nervousness' may well have owed
something to an over-taxed digestion. Coleridge found her
'a good innocent woman, as ever lived, but doleful as a dull
Tragedy', and wrote of her entertainingly but without much
sympathy.

Lady Beaumont's Sister (Mrs Fermor) left Bristol for Bath
yesterday – Poor afflicted Dowager! she clings obstinately to the
Faith, that the whole Source of her Sufferings is in her Head &
Heart, tho' it is evident that the mischief lies a foot or two below
the one, & 8 or 9 inches below the other –. For tho' 'alimentary
canal' & the 'lower digestive and eliminative organs' are handsome-
looking synonimes for Guts, yet they cannot stand the competition
with Desertion from Heaven, want of genial Grace, the *mind*, Sir!
O the *mind* –

Yet the friendship stood the long strains imposed upon it,
and the year before death broke it Coleridge is still able to
write of his earnest desire for a long evening spent in their
society, and Beaumont is still his ideal of 'a perfect gentleman'
. . . as Edmund Spenser sang, and Sidney realized the idea'.

With Wordsworth the friendship flowed on always deep
and clear, untroubled by suspicion or misunderstanding. There
was no guest more welcome, whether at London or Coleorton,
and the verses even now to be seen on a stone in Coleorton
grounds still speak of one of the richest friendships in all
that gifted circle, poet and artist united in affection 'by interchange of knowledge and delight'.

CHAPTER IX

Coleorton

Coleorton with its garden – the story of the Beaumonts and their friends keeps returning to this one beloved spot. It was the quiet centre of the last twenty years of the Beaumonts' happy life together, the place where they were most themselves. William Owen[1] found Sir George better company there than in town, 'very entertaining – playful, even Boyish'; while Lady Beaumont, charming London hostess though she was, moved more serenely in the quiet rhythms of country life that so well suited her gentle and reflective disposition. Their many guests there were as free as themselves, and every account of life at Coleorton breathes the same sense of ease within an informal comfortably ordered pattern.

Sir George would rise at 7.0 and walk in his beloved garden before the family breakfast at 8.30. There was comfortable social talk, and then Lady Beaumont would withdraw to her household cares or her reading, while her husband went straight to his painting room at the top of the house, or outside with easel and canvas. He would work all morning, until at 2.0 the horses were brought to the door and, wet or fine, he would go riding accompanied by any guests who cared for the exercise. At 5.0 came dinner, after which Lady Beaumont would sometimes read aloud from Cowper or her favourite Wordsworth, or Sir George would 'read a play in a manner the most delightful', or they would turn over with their guests part of the rich collection of portfolios of prints

---

[1] William Owen, R.A. (1769–1825), in 1813 appointed Principal Portrait Painter to the Prince Regent, but declined a Knighthood. He met an unfortunate end: laxative and opium were both prescribed for him during an illness; the apothecary accidentally mixed the labels, and Owen died through drinking a whole phial of the latter.

and drawings, or discuss the technicalities of painters' problems, studying the effects of candle-light or how best to paint the flame. (One remembers how often Coleridge was preoccupied by candle-flame, and Davy too. Its living, variable light was more conducive to speculation than the flat glare of electricity, even if less efficient.) At 9.0 the servants brought in fruit and a decanter of water, and at 11.0 the company retired for the night. On Sunday evenings the routine was a little varied by family prayers with the servants after dinner, a practice which 'highly gratified' the Presbyterian Wilkie, who had not encountered it elsewhere in England.

The hospitality of the new Hall was freely extended, and its spacious comfort greatly impressed those who came. Visitors delighted in surroundings which abounded, as Hearne said, with the picturesque – the woods, the rocks of Charnwood, the ruins of Grace Dieu. And then too there was all the interest attached to the laying out of grounds.

It is singularly fitting that the names of Wordsworth and Constable should be so closely linked by the garden as well as by their common friendship for its owners, for of all the brilliant Beaumont circle they were the two who best understood each other's work and whose freshness of vision had most effect upon Sir George himself and, through him, upon the world of cultivated taste. Unlike Wilkie, Constable listened with attentive pleasure as Lady Beaumont read to him from *The Excursion*, and found the landscape descriptions very beautiful. As he listened he must have recognized a spirit closely akin to his own. Both poet and painter depict nature with feelings closely similar, a sense of reverence, an awareness of distinct and brooding life, of inward joy. Their work is complementary, the same statement in different media. The dazzle of silver light in *The Hay Wain*, the warm shadows and the sunlit distance, are the 'green summer' of Wordsworth's poetry, felt with the same intensity, the same personal identification with the scene. To read Wordsworth or to look at a Constable is to be aware not only of familiar objects but of 'something far more deeply intertused', the landscape of inward vision fused with the visible scene itself. Appearances are only the visual expression of an intense secret vitality, and no art must be allowed to 'blind our eyes, and to prevent us from seeing the sun shine – the fields bloom – the trees blossom – and from hearing the foliage rustle'. This is the very quality of Wordsworth's vision also.

> *All things that love the sun are out of doors;*
> *The sky rejoices in the morning's birth;*
> *The grass is bright with rain-drops; – on the moors*
> *The hare is running races in her mirth;*
> *And with her feet she from the plashy earth*
> *Raises a mist, that, glittering in the sun,*
> *Runs with her all the way, wherever she doth run.*

There is a moral force in the natural scene itself, because man is both a part of the ordered world of nature, and yet a spiritual being distinct from it: and this also Wordsworth and Constable express in the same way, in the human figures, solitary and impressive, emerging from a landscape in which they seem almost to have grown like trees. Constable's Traveller rests on the shady verge beside an empty road, a shepherd pipes in the lonely silence of Dedham Vale, a woman carries her baby along the deserted track below the great trees that dwarf her – each seeming, like Wordsworth's old Cumberland beggar in his 'vast solitude', 'to breathe and live but for himself alone', living and dying in the light of Nature. Painter and poet are alike too in their sensitivity to minutest things, whether Constable's exquisite study of common poppies by the road side, or Wordsworth's linnet whose own flutterings create the 'shadows and sunny glimmerings that cover him all over'.

What more fitting and intimate a memorial than a garden to link together two such spirits with that of so good a friend? Here the new romantic spirit in poetry and art met and merged with the classical tradition in a form which even the least

aesthetic visitor to Coleorton could understand. For this was
the period in which gardening was one of the fine arts, even
if a minor one, and was practised by every gentleman with
the smallest claim to taste, whether he had an estate of
20,000 acres or of two. La Rochefoucald, visiting England in
1784, was much struck with the beauty of English parks and
pleasure grounds, though with a very French reservation as
to our incompetence in the vegetable garden. After describing the great landscape gardens, he is charmed and a
little amused by their modest counterparts.

Such gentlemen as are not rich enough to have parks have what is
called a lawn, a small stretch of land round the house with a number
of narrow paths, beautiful turf, and a little clump of trees, the whole
being kept with extreme tidiness. They design these little pleasure
grounds themselves. It is all they need to give them a sense of
proprietorship and to provide them with a walk for half an hour
before dinner.

The passion for landscape gardens had grown in the
Augustan peace of the eighteenth century, when the great
families amassed wealth and leisure enough for cultivated
domestic pursuits. To show his taste became the first social
necessity for a gentleman, and to show it he rebuilt his house,
hung it with paintings, and redesigned his grounds. To 'be in
earth and mortar' put him on the social map, and provided
an expensive and desirable hobby.

William Kent first made popular the landscape garden
which, though designed with the utmost care, should seem
the work of nature and would blend so well with the surrounding countryside that the boundary between them could
hardly be observed. 'Kent leaped the fence,' said Horace
Walpole, 'and saw that all nature was a garden.' The endless
but varied green of lawns and trees and natural vales, the
sunken ha-ha which takes the eye straight on to the tree-
shaded pasture beyond the lawns – these still exist at Rousham
just as they were designed by Kent in 1740, to show us what

Augustan taste once was. Lancelot ('Capability') Brown, who worked with Kent on the famous gardens of Stowe, carried his ideas still further. He received his nickname because he always 'considered the capabilities' of the grounds as to which he was consulted; but one is not quite sure of Jane Austen's tone of voice when her Mr Crawford 'was the first to move forward to examine the capabilities of that end of the house'. Brown's designs have sometimes a grandiose air, a too great ostentation of the magnificence of the house, that would have tempted her sense of irony. Winding streams, spanned by Palladian bridges, lakes, groups of trees, 'prospects' leading towards classical temples, these were the usual features of his landscapes. Our own generation, privileged to see the superb gardens of Wilton or Prior Park or Stourhead, fully matured and beautifully maintained, can but wonder at the imagination which could foresee in a shaven, newly planted desert, the exquisite contrasts in shape and colour of the garden to come, and at the disinterested enthusiasm which planted chiefly for posterity. But the landowners of the late eighteenth century, seeing the long straight avenues which were the glory of the Jacobean garden laid level with the ground, began to have their doubts as to the style which

wrapt all o'er in everlasting green,
Makes one dull, vapid, smooth, and tranquil scene.

Richard Payne Knight, who thus laments in his long didactic poem, *The Landscape* (1794), curses the 'haggard fiend' of this purely classical eighteenth-century park, the 'thin, meagre genius of the bare and bald'. He and his friend Sir Uvedale Price,[1] the Herefordshire squire of Foxley – both of them acquaintances of Beaumont – discussed interminably, in print and out of it, what should be the principles of taste in gardening. Change was in the air. Current taste was very strongly influenced by the paintings of Beaumont's adored Claude, to

[1] Sir Uvedale Price (1747–1829), author of *An Essay on the Picturesque*, 1794. Both Beaumont and Wordsworth were acquainted with him.

whom English artists, English patrons, and English landscape
gardeners were all equally devoted. Sir Kenneth Clark speaks
of 'the two chief lessons of Claude, that the centre of a landscape is an area of light, and that everything must be sub-
ordinate to a single mood'. One has only to walk by the lake
at Stourhead to see how his principles have been translated
into living growth, how skilfully vista gives way to vista, but
every one focused upon a patch of sky or silver trees or
stone temple, flanked always by the dense shadow of darker
growth.

Not even the irascible Payne Knight dared utter against
Claude. But he was one of the many who became bored by the
uniform greenness of a truly Claudian landscape. The fashion
now was to aim at Burke's 'sublime', even if one must be
content with a waterfall instead of a cataract, a grove of pine
trees rather than a wood. Above all, a garden must be
'picturesque'. The picturesque depends upon as much variety
as space will allow, and in its intention is wholly of the new
romantic school of thought. It is summed up by William
Gilpin, the high priest of the cult, who made travels in pursuit of picturesque scenery the newest enthusiasm, and who
produced essays and poems and portfolios of sketches to
propagate his ideas.

We are most delighted, when some grand scene . . . rising before
the eye, strikes us beyond the power of thought . . . and every
mental operation is suspended. In this pause of intellect; this
deliquium of the soul, an enthusiastic sensation of pleasure over-
spreads it, previous to any examination by the rules of art. The
general idea of the scene makes an impression, before any appeal
is made to the judgment. We rather *feel*, than *survey* it.

(Had Wordsworth been reading Gilpin just before he wrote
Tintern Abbey?) The new fashion coincides with the growing
taste for 'Gothic', so that many pseudo-medieval features
become desirable in gardens – 'ruins' that were never whole

buildings, ivied cottages in decay, rocks, dead branches, roots and moss, follies and hermit cells; and if one could employ a hermit actually to inhabit the cell or induce an owl to roost above it – at least while friends were being shown the garden – so much the better.

The extremes of romantic sensibility are a natural target for satire, and the gardening controversy provides the best of all opportunities for the anti-romantic, combining as it does the aestheticism of landscape design with that of art and poetry. Jane Austen, with the exquisite sense of balance which enables her to mock at the very romanticism that delights her, pokes sly fun at it in *Northanger Abbey*.

Catherine confessed and lamented her want of knowledge; declared that she would give anything in the world to be able to draw; and a lecture on the picturesque immediately followed, in which his instructions were so clear that she soon began to see beauty in everything admired by him; and her attention was so earnest that he became perfectly satisfied of her having a great deal of natural taste. He talked of foregrounds, distances, and second distances; side-screens and perspectives; lights and shades; – and Catherine was so hopeful a scholar, that when they gained the top of Beechen Cliff, she voluntarily rejected the whole city of Bath, as unworthy to make part of a landscape.

Jane Austen's fellow-novelist, Peacock, caricatures the arguments of Price and Payne Knight in a delicious scene in *Headlong Hall* where Sir Patrick O'Prism, 'a dilettante painter of high renown' (could this be a side-hit at Sir George himself?), discusses the grounds of the hall with Mr Milestone.

'For what is beautiful? That which pleases the eye. And what pleases the eye? Tints variously broken and blended. Now, tints variously broken and blended constitute the picturesque.'

'Allow me,' said Mr Gall: 'I distinguish the picturesque and the beautiful, and I add to them, in the laying out of grounds, a third and distinct character, which I call *unexpectedness*.'

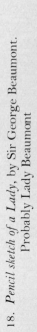

19. *George Dance, R.A.*, by John Jackson

18. *Pencil sketch of a Lady*, by Sir George Beaumont.
Probably Lady Beaumont

20. *Summer Morning in the Vale of Dedham*, by John Constable

'Pray, sir,' said Mr Milestone, 'by what name do you distinguish this character, when a person walks round the grounds for the second time?'

But though romantic sensibility might be laughed at, it could not be laughed away. Its very critics are a little in love with it. Anthelia, 'the mountain-enthusiast, the really romantic unworldly' heroine of Peacock's *Melincourt*, is a Wordsworthian Lucy who slips from the world of satire into that of poetry.

The majestic forms and wild energies of Nature that surrounded her from her infancy impressed their character on her mind, communicating to it all their own wildness, and more than their own beauty. Far removed from the pageantry of courts and cities, her infant attention was awakened to spectacles more interesting and more impressive; the misty mountain-top, the ash-fringed precipice; the gleaming cataract, the deep and shadowy glen, and the fantastic magnificence of the mountain clouds. The murmur of the woods, the rush of the winds, and the tumu·' ious dashing of the torrents, were the first music of her childhood.

Mrs Radcliffe could have written that with perfectly serious intent, and we should not have smiled; and when Anthelia seeks her favourite retreat we are charmed into forgetfulness of mockery.

An ash had fixed its roots in the fissures of the rock, and the knotted base of its aged trunk offered to the passenger a natural seat, over-canopied with its beautiful branches and leaves, now tinged with their autumnal yellow. . . . There was no breath of wind, no humming of insects, only the dashing of the waters beneath. She felt the presence of the genius of the scene. She sat absorbed in a train of contemplations dimly defined, but infinitely delightful: emotions rather than thoughts, which attention would have utterly dissipated, if it had paused to seize their images.

A devotee of Gilpin could hardly have bettered that, as a description of the effects of the picturesque upon a romantic imagination.

Such was the reigning taste when, in 1805, the Beaumonts began to consult Wordsworth about the new gardens at Coleorton. Wordsworth took the matter with becoming seriousness.

Laying out grounds, as it is called, may be considered as a liberal art, in some sort like poetry and painting; and its object, like that of all the liberal arts, is, or ought to be, to move the affections under the control of good sense.

As good sense includes an enlightened social consciousness, it prompts one major divergence from the principles of earlier landscape gardening. Those grounds designed by Kent and Brown were superb settings for the magnificence of great houses, to which the eye was by every means directed; but

nothing of that lofty or imposing interest, formerly attached to large property in land, can now exist; none of the poetic pride, pomp, and circumstance; nor anything that can be considered as making amends for violation done to the holiness of Nature.

True taste can find no fault with the landowner whose house belongs to the countryside rather than dominates it, who shows his good sense in the prosperity of his farms and the happiness of his tenants, and 'keeps himself as much out of sight as possible'.

A whole world of social, moral, and aesthetic change is here. It is the obtrusive mansion in palatial grounds which Constable has in mind when he complains that a gentleman's park is his aversion. There is no such ostentation at Coleorton. The square, elegant house appears to advantage if approached by the main drive, but from elsewhere in the park tall trees shut out the view of it, and the eye is led only to vistas of grass and leaves. The greater part of the grounds was laid out as a landscape garden in an unpretentious style. The area is too dry for lakes and serpentine streams, and the taste for small groups of trees islanded in wide sweeps of lawn was on the decline. Coleorton relies upon greenness, the smooth uprights of tree trunks against soft grass or darker shrubberies and spaces opening to the wide Leicestershire uplands beyond the park, which in Sir George's time were mostly moorland and wood. But nearer the house a pleasure ground was needed where Lady Beaumont could take the air at all times of the year, a sheltered 'winter garden' such as the *Spectator* had once described. This was the task which Wordsworth undertook during the long winter at the Coleorton farmhouse.

The area he had to work in was a small disused quarry, containing two great piles of rubbish left there by the builders. It was as well that the sphere of his activities was so strictly and clearly limited, for looming ominously over them was the head gardener, Mr Craig. Wilkie, painting in the winter garden three years later, was visited by an old gardener whom he 'found to be a Scotsman and a rather intelligent person', and received grave approval. But Wordsworth lacked the advantage of being a fellow Scot, and his amateur's enthusiasm was obviously met with severe reserve. Dorothy believes that Mr Craig 'may be inwardly rather petted; for he gives no *opinion* whatever; and we had long ago found out that his character was exactly what you describe – very obstinate and somewhat self-conceited; withal industrious, ingenious, and faithful'. Wordsworth did his best to be tactful. He praised Mr Craig's new walk, embowered with roses and bramble, went with him to buy plants, and took his advice on the pool to be made in the winter garden. Poet and gardener worked in a cautious truce. Wordsworth reports to Lady Beaumont that Mr Craig has lately 'seemed fully preoccupied; and, to speak the truth, as he has very cheerfully given up the winter garden to my control, I do not like to intermeddle much with the other'.

Wordsworth's completed plan was the epitome of the romantic mood. The whole stress is on feeling, the stirring of the 'affections'. The area was to be surrounded by evergreen shrubs, cypress and firs, 'to give it the greatest appearance of depth, shelter, and seclusion', and within it was to be as much of the picturesque as the small space could contain. The rubbish heaps were to be planted with shrubs, trees, and flowers. A shaded alley, flanked by evergreens, was to provide refreshment in times of heat or protection in winter cold, its floor being firm but lightly covered with moss, 'so that the whole would be still, unvaried, and cloistral, soothing but not stirring the mind, or tempting it out of itself'. Where the garden was bounded by the new wall of the terrace above there were to be ivy and pyracanthus, and flower borders filled chiefly with a great variety of spring and autumn flowers, but elsewhere the only flowers would be the wild ones, such as periwinkle and primroses – his early favourites.

> Through primrose tufts in that green bower
> The periwinkle trails its leaves.

Elsewhere would be a holly hedge (remembered perhaps from that at Alfoxden), a thicket and a grove, open glades, and a bower 'such as you will find described in the beginning of Chaucer's poem of *The Flower and the Leaf*, and also in the beginning of *The Assembly of Ladies*'. He had visions of a fountain or *jet d'eau* – an old-fashioned taste about which he was a little apologetic – but Mr Craig had the grim satisfaction of telling him that there was insufficient water in the area. But a wych elm grew beside an old flight of steps at the boundary of the garden, and here he contrived a trickle of water about the roots, where there might be 'vivid masses of water-plants, a refreshing and beautiful sight in the dead time of the year, and which, when cased in ice, form one of the most enchanting appearances that are peculiar to winter'. (One hears a faint echo of Cowper, and perhaps of *Kubla Khan*.)

Along the boundary were two cottages in suitably romantic decay, which should most certainly be retained. One was already covered in ivy, while the other had such an 'irregular and picturesque form' that its unsightly surface was to be repaired and covered with trailing plants until it also could support an ivy grove. Finally there was to be an 'image' created by little glade which summed up the intention of the whole.

In this little glade should be a basin of water inhabited by two gold or silver fish, if they will live in this climate all the year in the open air; if not, any others of the most radiant colours that are the most hardy; these little creatures to be the 'genii' of the pool and of the place. This spot should be as monotonous in the colour of the trees as possible. The enclosure of evergreen, the sky above, the green grass floor, and the two mute inhabitants, the only images it should present, unless here and there a solitary wild flower.

This is the very essence of a Regency garden in the latest taste. Its mood is literary. It is no longer to be an elegantly contrived sublimation of the surrounding landscape, dominated by the great house for which it is the setting. It is a spot remote and retired, a place to stir reflection and promote poetic thought. Visitors to Coleorton who could make little of Mr Wordsworth's poetry would fully appreciate his garden and understand the principles on which he had planned it, for gardening had indeed become the 'liberal art' which every educated man or woman could profess. Its importance to the ordinary cultivated person is clearly evident in Jane Austen's novels. She describes her scenes in so easy and un-affected a manner that one can overlook their significance; yet she uses pleasure grounds as a measure of the taste and understanding of the owner, and even on occasion as an assignment of just desert. Donwell Abbey is an admirable example of a modest gentleman's seat. It is not quite perfect, for Mr John Knightley, 'domestic and respectable' though he was, had faults which hardly entitled him to *absolute* happiness; but it had picturesque variety which is described with some-thing of Constable's affection for the mere Englishness of the scene.

They followed one another to the delicious shade of a broad avenue of limes, which, stretching beyond the garden at an equal distance from the river, seemed the finish of the pleasure grounds. It led to nothing; nothing but a view at the end over a low stone wall with high pillars, which seemed intended, in their erection, to give the appearance of an approach to the house, which had never been there. Disputable, however, as might be the taste of such a termination, it was in itself a charming walk, and the view which closed it extremely pretty. The considerable slope, at nearly the foot of which the Abbey stood, gradually acquired a steeper form beyond its grounds; and at half a mile distant was a bank of considerable abruptness and grandeur, well clothed with wood; and at the bottom of this bank, favourably placed and sheltered, rose the Abbey Mill Farm with meadows in front, and the river making a close and handsome curve around it.

It was a sweet view – sweet to the eye and the mind. English verdure, English culture, English comfort, seen under a sun bright, without being oppressive.

Emma's brother-in-law must have grounds of whose 'respectability' at least there can be no doubt. But when a vain and tiresome girl makes a match with a dull, stupid, and rather ill-bred young man, of whom his creator thoroughly disapproves, she must acquire the grounds she deserves. Sotherton, Mr Rushworth's seat in *Mansfield Park*, gave evidence of wealth, but it was old-fashioned and lacked both imagination and taste.

The situation of the house excluded the possibility of much prospect from any of the rooms. . . . Every room on the west front looked across a lawn to the beginning of the avenue immediately beyond tall iron palisades and gates. . . . The lawn, bounded on each side by a high wall, contained beyond the first planted area a bowling-green, and beyond the bowling-green a long terrace walk, backed by iron palisades, and commanding a view over them into the tops of the trees of the wilderness immediately adjoining. It was a good spot for fault-finding.

A considerable flight of steps landed them in the wilderness, which was a planted wood of about two acres, and though chiefly of larch and laurel, and beech cut down, and though laid out with too much regularity, was darkness and shade, and natural beauty, compared with the bowling-green and the terrace. They all felt the refreshment of it.

Poor Maria Bertram, who deserved a garden containing 'a good spot for fault-finding'. But when Elizabeth Bennet, surely Jane Austen's own favourite, sees her destined home for the first time, it is as near perfection as any estate could be.

The park was very large and contained great variety of ground. They entered it in one of its lowest points, and drove for some time through a beautiful wood stretching over a wide extent. . . .

They gradually ascended for half a mile, and then found themselves at the top of a considerable eminence, where the wood ceased, and the eye was instantly caught by Pemberley House, situated on the opposite side of a valley, into which the road with some abruptness wound. It was a large handsome stone building, standing well on rising ground, and backed by a ridge of high woody hills; and in front, a stream of some natural importance was swelled into greater, but without any artificial appearance. Its banks were neither formal nor falsely adorned. Elizabeth was delighted. She had never seen a place for which nature had done more, or where natural beauty had been so little counteracted by an awkward taste.

It might almost be a description of Constable's *Englefield House*; and what more could any heroine deserve than this charming and reasonable blend of the best of established eighteenth-century taste in landscape with the picturesque qualities of romanticism?

All that Coleorton stood for in the mind of its owner, all the inheritance of classical taste, and all the romanticism of Wordsworth and Constable, is immortalized in *The Cenotaph*. The memorial to Reynolds, inscribed by Wordsworth, flanked by the busts on their stone pedestals, is in the full vein of eighteenth-century sentiment, while over all the lime trees form a pleasing and romantic gloom; the picturesque stag in the foreground suggests the mood of a Shakespearean glade and even reminds one of Sir George's own picture of *Jacques and the Stag*, now in the vaults of the National Gallery. When *The Cenotaph* was finally exhibited, in 1836, Constable wrote to a friend that he 'preferred to see Sir Joshua Reynolds' name and Sir George Beaumont's once more in the catalogue, for the last time at the old house'.

It was a conjunction which Sir George, had he been still alive, would have found peculiarly happy.

21. *The Cenotaph*, by John Constable

22. *The Blind Fiddler*, by Sir David Wilkie

23. *Landscape with Jacques and the Wounded Stag*, by Sir George Beaumont

CHAPTER X

The Public Benefactor

Sir George Beaumont's love of art was complex, absolute, and dedicated. He loved it as himself a practioner, as the friend of genius, the patron of any promising talent, the connoisseur whose judgment was sought and flattered, and the collector whose pictures were his daily happiness. His love was a disinterested passion, and the desire to share it with all who wished lay very close to his heart. The generosity of connoisseurs was not enough: only the fortunate few could see their treasures. Public exhibitions lasted but a short time and could be viewed only by those who happened to be in London. Beaumont began to cherish a dream, the possibility of a national gallery of pictures which should belong to the public and not to the private collector.

Meanwhile he encouraged the knowledge of pictures among ordinary people by the only means then available, the use of engravings. Engravers had been among his own earliest friends in 'the Art', and he was generous in permitting his own pictures to be so copied, whether his own compositions, those commissioned from contemporary artists, or in his collection of Old Masters. The sale of the prints profited both the engraver and the artist and was another means by which the patron could support both.

Sir George was always happy to encourage local men. His own pictures were sometimes engraved by John Browne of Finchingfield, not far from Dunmow. He may have met him when he was for a time apprenticed to William Woollett; certainly an engraving of his from Beaumont's picture, *The Forest*, was exhibited at the Royal Academy in 1801. Browne was a gifted draughtsman, whom Blake thought superior to his master. 'Woollett's best works were etched by Jack Browne; Woollett etched very ill himself.' Certainly Blake disliked Woollett as 'a heavy lump of ignorance and cunning'; but he was himself too pure an artist to let his personal feelings touch his integrity as a judge of other men's work.

In 1807 Edward Forster, chaplain to the Duke of Newcastle, initiated the *British Gallery of Engravings* from pictures owned by the king and other private collectors. His advertisement for it is a characteristic example of British self-congratulation during the troubles of Europe after the French Revolution.

From the many important events and singular changes, which have taken place in different parts of Europe, during the last twenty years, England has derived at least one advantage; namely, the possession of some of the finest Pictures in the world. The dispersion of most of the different Galleries and Collections, in Italy, France and Germany, has enabled the admirers of the Fine Arts, in this country, to acquire the purest specimens of the greatest Masters: and we can now boast of larger and more valuable collections than were ever known in Great Britain.

Sir George, who thought the English collections far inferior to those in Europe, would not have agreed with him in this, but he would support any plan that might spread the knowledge of his darling art, and his name is in the prospectus among those who had given permission to have their pictures engraved. It added cachet to the list, for he was already an acknowledged authority, one of the half dozen whose names recur whenever there is any public matter relating to art. In 1802 he was appointed to a Treasury committee entrusted to commission war memorials, which decided that Flaxman was to undertake Admiral Howe's; Banks, Captain Westcott's; Westmacott, General Abercrombie's; and Rossi, one for Captain Ross and Captain Riou.

Three years later, in April 1805, came a private meeting, initiated by another great patron of art, Sir Thomas Bernard[1], which was to affect the fortunes of many contemporary artists. West, the President of the Royal Academy, invited Sir George to attend, and Farington, William Smith, Payne Knight, Lawrence, and Smirke, were also present. Sir Thomas was to outline to them his plan for a national gallery and for encouraging historical painting. The first proposal was one close to Beaumont's heart, though he had his reservations about offering premiums for contemporary works. He spoke once to Farington of 'Artists making Patrons by the excellence of their productions, rather than of making artists by giving money, which would operate to create a vast increase of Artists raised in hopes of obtaining it'. The meeting brought a national gallery no nearer; probably there were others who shared Constable's view that if one should be founded 'there will be an end of the art in poor old England, and she will become, in all that relates to painting, as much a nonentity as every other country that has one. The reason is plain; the manufacturers of pictures are then made the criterions of perfection, instead of nature.'

Next month, however, came another meeting of famous patrons and artists, including many who had attended the previous discussion: and on May 13, 1805, it was resolved to found a British Institution for the encouragement of the arts, including their technical application to English manu-factures. Those who subscribed a hundred guineas to the project were to become 'hereditary governors', and Sir George of course was one of those. He also was one of the nine members voted on to the Select Committee to prepare a draft of regulations for the new Institution and to find a site for its activities. At a second meeting he was again nominated

---

[1] Sir Thomas Bernard (1750–1818), art collector, patron, philanthropist; Treasurer of the Foundling Hospital. He also promoted the foundation of the Fever Institution and a school for the indigent blind. In 1808 he founded a training school for teachers at Bishop Auckland, under the direct superinten-dence of Dr Bell.

to a further Select Committee to manage the concerns of the British Institution until Governors should be elected. The Shakespeare Gallery in Pall Mall was purchased as a permanent centre, and in due course Beaumont became one of the Directors of the Institute.

The avowed aims of the new body were characteristic of the age – on the one hand disinterested and 'sublime', to encourage artists 'to paint the mind and passions of man, to depicture his sympathies and affections, and to illustrate the great events which have been recorded in the history of the world'; on the other hand they smack already of nineteenth-century materialism, in that 'the Fine Arts essentially and abundantly contribute to the national prosperity and resources', and it is hoped that the founding of the Institute will give England an advantage in her relation to other countries. It was by no means intended as a rival to the Royal Academy, although in effect it often became so in the eyes of contemporary painters. When, for instance, the Academy hung Haydon's *Dentatus* in an anteroom, he was so piqued that he withdrew it and sent it to the British Institution instead. Annual premiums were offered for contemporary paintings (though not always awarded), and annual exhibitions were presented, sometimes of Old Masters, sometimes of contemporary art.

By this time Beaumont's influence was firmly established; and in March 1806 he was asked to join another committee to decide on the merits of the twenty-seven or twenty-eight models submitted for Lord Nelson's monument; but this time although he gained the support of other advisers to the committee, his own candidate, Rossi, failed to get the commission. It was given to James Smith instead, by a majority of the Common Council. West was one of those whose design was rejected, although the picture which he afterwards painted from it still exists in the Mellon Collection – an exuberantly allegorical mêlée of waves, cherubs, clouds, and seamen, surrounding Victory, who is taking Nelson's body from Neptune to present it to Britannia. Nelson, leprous-white and swathed in a white toga of some sort, is regarded with an expression of scandalized horror by a British lion clutching the titles of his victories; and the whole thing is mounted upon a sculptured and architectural base – thus uniting the three branches of art which constituted the Academy – and complicated by groups of seamen and marines. The committee may well have found the design more overwhelming than the artist intended. West's popularity was declining at the time, and there was even some talk that he might be removed from the Presidency of the Academy, although Sir George thought 'it would be a very ill-judged measure'. Henry Hope, the wealthy merchant and art collector, even suggested in private conversation that the Academy should have a President who was not a professional but a man of distinction such as Sir George Beaumont himself. The report of his remark got about, so others may have agreed with it, but Beaumont would have been the last to do so. For all the assurance that his rank and talent gave him, he was wholly without vanity and the desire of public place; nor would he have wished Sir Joshua's seat to be filled by any but the best of practising artists.

That early friend still held the place of honour in his heart, and in the summer of 1811 he conceived the idea of an exhibition devoted solely to his works. The idea of a one-man exhibition was an innovation, and it was another two years before he had persuaded his fellow Directors at the British Institution and completed the plans. But at last it was formally opened by a dinner given in June 1813, at which the Prince Regent himself was present. (Whatever his faults, George IV was a genuine supporter of art, as his father had been of music.) Constable was one of those invited, and was much impressed by the company as well as the pictures. Jane Austen too, in London at the time, visited the Reynolds Exhibition as well as one in Spring Gardens where, she wrote to her sister, she had been

very well pleased with a small portrait of Mrs Bingley, excessively
like her . . . size, shaped face, features, and sweetness; there never
was a greater likeness. She is dressed in a white gown, with green
ornaments, which convinces me of what I had always supposed,
that green was a favourite colour with her. I dare say Mrs D.
will be in yellow.

Later in the same day she reports that she and her brother
Henry have now visited the Royal Academy and the Reynolds
Exhibition but, alas, found Mrs Darcy in neither.

I can only imagine that Mr Darcy prizes any picture of her too
much to like it should be exposed to the public eye. I can imagine he
would have that sort of feeling – that mixture of love, pride, and
delicacy.

But had she looked close enough she might have seen two
young, elegant creatures, the young woman a little solemn
and naïve, who might well have been Anne Elliot and Captain Wentworth (had the gentleman been in uniform) in the
days of their first courtship – he 'a remarkably fine young
man, with a great deal of intelligence, spirit, and brilliancy
and she an extremely pretty girl, with gentleness, modesty,
taste and feeling': Sir Joshua's two wedding portraits of
Sir George and Lady Beaumont were among those loaned to
the exhibition.

The Reynolds pictures drew large crowds; and catalogues
of other annual exhibitions in the British Gallery show how
rich were the treasures lent by private owners. But there was
still no permanent gallery for the public, nor regular grants
of government money for the purchase of works of art. Sir
George felt that England was lagging behind other European
countries in her culture, and even as late as 1821 he was still
deploring her dearth of the greatest works of art. He wrote
from Rome to Lord Mulgrave:

For easil [?modern] pictures we can match the world, and thank
Heaven we have almost all the Claudes – But when we talk of

pictures of the grand Calibre – the very highest clap – we are poor indeed.

Meanwhile his own collection was accumulating, and all hope of a son to inherit it had long since faded. Title and estates would go to a little cousin, who was sometimes invited to stay, both at London and Coleorton. He was welcomed as the heir, and with much affection, but who could know whether he would share his relative's tastes in adult life. Sir George pondered his problem, and discussed it with Farington during that autumn visit in 1812 when the foundation of the Reynolds cenotaph was laid in the garden. They were riding out together to view the famous rocks at Charnwood when he broached the possibility of leaving his treasures to the nation. 'He thought that by placing fine pictures at a distance from the metropolis the public were deprived of a high gratification and a means of keeping up good taste.' Pictures left to one's heirs were exposed to the dangers attending changes of taste, or possible ignorance, carelessness, or financial necessity. They might be damaged by injudicious cleaning, stored away in harmful conditions, sold to pay off debts or to provide marriage portions. If he were now to present his pictures to the public, there was no fit place where they might safely be housed. But the thought had taken root and grew. The project of a National Gallery was never far from his mind and he discussed it with many men of influence.

He found a sympathetic supporter in the Hon George Agar Ellis, afterwards Lord Dover, who urged the project in the House of Commons, but nothing was done. Then he spoke of it to Lord Liverpool: 'Assure the Government that I will give my own pictures to the nation, as soon as there is a proper place allotted for their reception.' Liverpool was friendly, but hesitated at the expense, even though the Earl of Aberdeen and Lord Farnborough offered their support. Then, in 1823, the moment of choice was forced suddenly

K*

upon the government by the death of the great banker, John Julius Angerstein. Next to the Marquis of Stafford's, Angerstein's collection of pictures was probably the finest in the country, and it was strongly rumoured that both the King of Bavaria and the Emperor of Russia were interested in its purchase. At last the Treasury was forced to make a move.

Hansard reports the debate of July 1, 1823, when the report of the committee of supply was brought up. A resolution was moved that £40,000 be granted to the King for defraying the expense of buildings at the British Museum to house the Royal Library, left by George III to the nation. Mr Hobhouse at once suggested Whitehall as a more suitable repository, being 'averse to spending money upon such a piece of patchwork as the British Museum'. He was supported by Mr Croker, who 'thought the British Museum a very ill-contrived, inconvenient, insecure building'. The books might be left there in safety, but not the models and paintings.

This was the chance for which Beaumont's friends had been waiting. Sir Charles Long defended the Museum, but said 'room was certainly wanted; for Sir George Beaumont had offered his collection to the Museum, and it had been declined, for want of a place to put it in'.

Now Ellis was on his feet again, nervous of attack from the economists and, as he admitted later, lacking courage to press the subject were it not for Sir George's zeal, and permission to announce his donation to the country:

He praised the noble and patriotic gift of Sir George Beaumont. The collection of Mr Angerstein would be sold in the course of next year and, if not looked after, would very probably go out of the country. His intention was to move for a grant in the next session, to be applied, under commissioners, to the purchase of this and other collections, for the formation of a national gallery.

Mr Baring then pointed out the number of valuable works now in private hands, owing to the French Revolution, which must in the nature of things return again to the great cabinets and collections. And really, for a country of such inordinate wealth and power as this to be without a gallery of art, was a national reproach.

Faced with so much eloquence and high-mindedness the economists ceased to struggle, and the House passed Mr Croker's amendment, to place the design and expenditure of 'a suitable edifice for the reception of the several collections of the British Museum' and any works to be purchased later, under the control of the Treasury.

The National Gallery was founded.

The Archbishop of Canterbury wrote a formal letter of thanks to Sir George Beaumont, and the latter wrote to congratulate Ellis on his success.

I hope you will pardon my troubling you with my congratulations. By easy access to such works of art, the public taste must improve, which I think the grand desideratum; for when the time shall come when bad pictures, or even works of mediocrity, shall be neglected, and excellence never passed over, my opinion is, we shall have fewer painters, and better pictures. I think the public already begin to feel works of art are not merely toys for connoisseurs, but solid objects of concern to the nation; and those who consider it in the narrowest point of view, will perceive that works of high excellence pay ample interest for the money they cost. My belief is, that the Apollo, the Venus, the Laocoön, &c, are worth thousands a year to the country which possesses them.

Angerstein's collection was bought for the nation. The solid, heavy-jowled banker still lives for us in Reynolds' portrait. He stands in his red coat with something of the potentially dangerous energy of a quiet bull, and one can glimpse the quality which brought a mere underwriter at Lloyds to the control of a princely fortune. He would have liked the tribute paid him three years after his death in William Miller's *Biographical Sketches of British Characters Recently Deceased.*

Let not, therefore, the pride of high Nobility cast a word of contempt at the British Trader; for here is one who not only increased the wealth, but contributed to improve the taste, promote the arts, and embellish the public walls of his Country.

But grateful as we may be to the British Trader – and he deserved the capital letters – Haydon's last words on Sir George give the real credit.

For though Angerstein's pictures were a great temptation, yet without Sir George Beaumont's offer of his own collection, it is a question if they would have been purchased. He is justly entitled to be considered as the founder of the National Gallery. . . . Let him be crowned. Peace to him.

In 1826 Sir George handed over his own collection of pictures to the British Museum, to be transferred in time to the new Gallery. He asked only that one might be returned to him for the period of his life: the *Hagar and the Angel*, best loved of all his Claudes (no. 61 in the National Gallery today), was with him to the last.

CHAPTER XI

Epilogue

The founding of the National Gallery had been the crowning achievement of Sir George's life as a patron of the arts, and with it he must have felt his work was done. An autumnal tone has begun to mist the records of the years immediately preceding it. Both he and Lady Beaumont were in delicate health. William Owen reports a meeting with the latter in 1818, when

he thought her much altered in her appearance – that she looked worn and old. – He thought her to be 62 or 63 years old. I told him she was not more than 60. – He sd. she spoke in a desponding way – that for 30 years she & Sir George had breakfasted together, but that of late from indisposition in one or the other of them this had been interrupted. He sd. her visit to him was like that of one coming to take leave.

Yet there were contented and peaceful times still to come, such as the last long visit to Italy in 1821, when Sir George wrote long, happy, charming letters to the Mulgraves, describing every stage of the journey. They crossed the Channel by the new-fangled steamboat, which they thoroughly disapproved.

Its only advantage and a great one to be sure is your security with regard to time, but by waiting for passengers they commonly contrive to make you lose your tide; and as to sickness, tho we had fine weather, I never knew the mortality greater.

Travelling from Paris in their own carriage, unfortunately up-to-date enough to open at the top, he caught 'one of his slow fevers' – but recovered enough to enjoy Lausanne, where they unexpectedly encountered the Kembles and Mrs Siddons. Their spirits rose as they approached their beloved Italy, and from the foot of the Simplon Pass saw 'the whole range of the Alps, set in such a day of crystal, as I shall not attempt to describe'. He delighted in Verona with its 'atmosphere clear beyond description and saturated with ultramarine', while the paintings at Venice and Mantua made him 'tipsy with colour'. They braved the road to Naples unescorted, despite reports of brigands, and, reaching it safely, arrived just in time to see an eruption of Vesuvius, 'the most magnificent firework I ever saw'.

Most fittingly this last Italian journey contained both a triumph and a threnody. Reaching Rome, Sir George made his last lavish purchase of a great work of art, one indeed 'of the very highest clap' – the unfinished bas-relief by Michelangelo of the Virgin and Child with St John. The Italian sculptor, Canova, tenderly supervised its despatch, and it was received by the English sculptor, Chantrey. Sir George asked that no one else might see it until his own return, when it was hung for a brief and splendid period above the great staircase at Coleorton, until his heir presented it to the Royal Academy. The beauty of the infant Christ woke in him that wistful interest in childhood which showed itself so often in these two childless people, and his thoughts turned to that earliest friend who had so often caught its charm.

One would almost imagine Sir Joshua had seen it (he wrote to Chantrey): the child has much of that transient grace so common to children, the hitting of which he calls shooting flying.

But in Rome also he sought in vain the scene of an earlier pilgrimage. Since his first visit there the French Republican troops had devastated Italy; soldiers quartered in Rome had turned out the Convent of the Fratri Minori to make a barracks of the church of the Trinita al Monte. Within the church had been the monument to Claude Lorrain, erected by his nephews, and had he found even the fragments of it Sir George would have brought them home to the little church at Coleorton. But the monument to his most beloved painter was wholly obliterated.

The Beaumonts loitered in Italy until the spring of the next year. They still 'had the most sanguine hopes of seeing it again'; but when Wilkie went abroad in 1823 in the hope of recovering his health, Sir George confessed that he felt the effects of age increasing every year and that his wife's health had grown delicate, so that they dare not risk the journey. Instead they enjoyed the retirement of Coleorton or visits to friends such as the Lonsdales at Lowther or the Mulgraves at Whitby. An alliance was arranged for the young cousin, George Howland Willoughby Beaumont, who would one day succeed to the baronetcy. One feels that they were relaxing their hold upon life's business, though never upon friendship.

Sir George had travelled a long way in his seventy-four years, a journey that bridged the whole distance from the elegant repose of mid-eighteenth-century taste, with its wise tension between reason, intellect, and imagination, its appeal to common principles and common experience, to the intense individualism of the romantic period of Wordsworth and Coleridge, with its stress on personal feelings and inward vision. One of his latest letters to his lifelong friend, Lord Mulgrave, reveals how closely Beaumont became identified with Wordsworthian modes of thought. He had just left the Mulgraves and was on his way from Whitby to Castle Howard, when he experienced the beauty of moorland scenery.

It was not possible to quit such dear friends without a heartfelt pang, which was both soothed and increased by the scenery alternately cheerful & solemn which I had to pass before I plunged into the moors. What a change! Yet their desolation is sublime, & I can imagine a composition might be formed from them which by the assistance of appropriate figures would make a striking picture, which would impress the mind of the spectator with awe and not unpleasing melancholy – But then the painter must be a poet – a mere matter of fact man can never give sentiment to his landscapes.

This was in the autumn of 1826. On February 7, 1827, Sir George walked for the last time in the grounds of Coleorton. When he returned to the house he shivered and complained of cold. Erisypilis broke out upon his head – a disease from which at that time there was little hope of recovery – and in a few hours he was dead.

Margaret Beaumont outlived him only by two years. In her old age she had grown somewhat sharp-tongued in her political sympathies. Crabb Robinson[1] had found her 'a fine old lady and very lively, but bitter against the Whigs . . . disposed to be as intolerant as politeness would permit'. But politics apart, she had lost none of that early charm. He thought her 'a gentlewoman of great sweetness and dignity . . . among the most interesting by far of the persons of quality in the country'. Perhaps only Dorothy Wordsworth fully understood her desolation on her husband's death, and she was with her as often as she could be.

Sir George's kindnesses outlived him in remembrances to his friends, such as the £100 he left to Wilkie, and the yearly pension of the same sum to Wordsworth so that he and his sister might still sometimes afford a holiday; in actual fact it made up a fifth of their income. Many spoke of his death with genuine grief, but Sir Walter Scott's reception of the news, detached, almost impersonal, gives as true a picture as any.

Sir George Beaumont's dead; by far the most sensible and pleasing man I ever knew – kind, too, in his nature, and generous – gentle in society, and of those mild manners which tend to soften

---

[1] Henry Crabb Robinson (1775–1867), one of the first of foreign correspondents, subsequently editor of *The Times*. His voluminous diary and correspondence give interesting glimpses of many of his contemporaries.

the causticity of the general London tone of persiflage and personal satire. As an amateur painter, he was of the very highest distinction; and though I know nothing of the matter, yet I should hold him a perfect critic on painting, for he always made his criticisms intelligible, and used no slang. I am very sorry – as much as it is in my nature to be – for one whom I could see but seldom. He was the great friend of Wordsworth, and understood his poetry, which is a rare thing, for it is more easy to see his peculiarities than to feel his great merit, or follow his abstract ideas.

Scott was a year younger than Wordsworth, and for his generation it was true that to understand the latter's poetry was a rare thing. But in the readiness and depth of his comprehension Sir George helped others to appreciate it too. He had seen the end of one world and the beginning of a new. The quick astonishing harvest of the second generation of Romantic writers was already over – Keats, Byron, and Shelley were dead. The age of the private patron was over too, and Sir George himself with his new National Gallery had done something to end it; writer and artist now depended directly on a public that was largely middle class. In the year of Sir George's death a very young man called Alfred Tennyson published his first volume of poems. London University was founded in that same year, and Karl Marx was already nine years old. As the first passenger steam train clanked noisily on its way, watched by astonished gentleman in top hats and frock coats, the elegant age of the Beaumonts receded into the past.

Sir George Beaumont's Gift
to the National Gallery

Given according to the present catalogue. Titles and attributions given in brackets are those of the original presentation.

CAT. NO.	ARTIST	TITLE
19	Claude	*Landscape: Narcissus* (Narcissus and Echo)
40	Poussin	*Landscape: A Man Washing his Feet at a Fountain* (Landscape with Figures)
43	Rembrandt	*The Deposition*
51	Ascribed to Rembrandt (Rembrandt)	*A Seated Man with a Stick: 'A Jew Merchant'*
55	After Claude (Claude)	*Landscape: The Death of Procris*
58	Claude	*Landscape with a Goatherd and Goats*
61	Claude	*Landscape: Hagar and the Angel* (Landscape with Figures)
64	Bourdon	*The Return of the Ark*
66	Rubens	*The Château de Steen* (Autumn – The Château de Steen)
71	Both	*A Rocky Landscape with Herdsmen and Muleteers* (Landscape – Morning)
99	Wilkie	*The Blind Fiddler* [Tate Gallery]
106	Reynolds	*A Man's Head* [Tate Gallery]
108	Wilson	*Ruins of Villa of Maecenas* [Tate Gallery]
110	Wilson	*Niobe* [Transferred to Tate Gallery in 1919. Destroyed by enemy action 1939–45]
126	West	*Pylades and Orestes* [Tate Gallery]
127	Canaletto	*Venice: Campo S. Vidal and S. Maria della Carità* ('The Stone Mason's Yard')

Sources

(Dates are those of the editions I have used – not necessarily the original dates of publication)

HENRY ANGELO: *Reminiscences*: 1830.

EDMUND BURKE: *A Philosophical Enquiry into the Origin of our Ideas of the Sublime and the Beautiful*: 1756.

K. COBURN (Ed.): *The Notebooks of Samuel Taylor Coleridge*: 1957 –

ALLAN CUNNINGHAM: *Lives of the Most Eminent British Painters*: 1880.

ALLAN CUNNINGHAM: *Life of Sir David Wilkie*: 1843.

WILLIAM GILPIN: *An Essay on Picturesque Travel*: 1792.

J. GRIEG (Ed.): *The Farington Diary*: 1922.

E. L. GRIGGS (Ed.): *The Letters of Samuel Taylor Coleridge*: 1956.

WILLIAM HAZLITT: *The Conversations of James Northcote*: 1871.

R. P. KNIGHT: *The Landscape*: 1794.

W. KNIGHT (Ed.): *Memorials of Coleorton*: 1887.

LA ROCHEFOUCAULD: *A Frenchman in England,* 1784 (*Mélanges sur l'Angleterre*, trans. S. C. Roberts, 1933).

C. R. LESLIE: *Memoirs of the Life of John Constable* (Phaidon ed: 1951, text of 1845 ed.)

J. G. LOCKHART: *The Life of Sir Walter Scott*: 1850.

W. MILLER: *Biographical Sketches of British Characters Recently Deceased*: 1826.

PHILIP MORANT: *History and Antiquities of the County of Essex*: 1788.

E. J. MORLEY (Ed.): *Books and Their Writers: Henry Crabb Robinson*: 1938.

E. J. MORLEY (Ed.): *Correspondence of Crabb Robinson with the Wordsworth Circle*: 1927.

NICHOLS: *History of Leicestershire*: 1795.

SIR J. REYNOLDS: *Discourses*: 1842.

E. DE SELINCOURT (Ed.): *Early Letters of William and Dorothy Wordsworth*: 1935.

T. TAYLOR (Ed.): *Autobiography and Memoirs of J. R. Haydon*: 1926.

A. TRENEER: *The Mercurial Chemist*: 1963.
Universal British Directory: 1793.
Vesey Jun: Reports, 599 (Beaumont v. Boultbee).

W. T. WHITLEY: *Artists and their Friends in England*: 1928.

W. WING: *Annals of North Aston*: 1867.

Unpublished: Letters from Sir George Beaumont to Lord and Lady Mulgrave.

Index

(Page numbers in bold type refer to main entries)